ALSO BY KENNETH C. DAVIS

Picture books:

Don't Know Much About® the 50 States
Don't Know Much About® the Solar System

Middle-grade titles:

Don't Know Much About® Planet Earth

Adult titles:

Don't Know Much About® History
Don't Know Much About® Geography
Don't Know Much About® the Civil War
Don't Know Much About® the Bible
Don't Know Much About® the Universe

DON'T KNOW MUCH ABOUT®

SPACE

KENNETH C. DAVIS

ILLUSTRATED BY SERGIO RUZZIER

HarperCollins*Publishers*

Photo credits: page 31, © 1994 by Fred Espenak; page 54, courtesy of NASA/JPL, artwork by Donald E. Davis; page 63, courtesy of NASA/JPL; page 69, courtesy of NASA/JPL, artwork by Dave Seal; all other photos courtesy of NASA.

This is a Don't Know Much About® book. Don't Know Much About®
is the trademark of Kenneth C. Davis.

Don't Know Much About® Space

Library of Congress Cataloging-in-Publication Data
Davis, Kenneth C.
    Don't know much about space / by Kenneth C. Davis.
        p.   cm.
    Includes bibliographical references and index.
    ISBN 0-06-028601-6 — ISBN 0-06-028602-4 (lib. bdg.) — ISBN 0-06-440835-3 (pbk.)
    1. Astronomy—Juvenile literature.   [1. Astronomy—Miscellanea.   2. Questions and answers.]
I. Title.
QB46.D33   2001   00-069713
520—dc21

Design by Charles Yuen
2   3   4   5   6   7   8   9   10

First Edition

ACKNOWLEDGMENTS

An author's name goes on the cover of a book. But behind that book are a great many people who make it all happen. I would like to thank all of the wonderful people at HarperCollins who helped make this book a reality, including Susan Katz, Kate Morgan Jackson, Barbara Lalicki, Harriett Barton, Rosemary Brosnan, Meredith Charpentier, Anne Dunn, Dana Hayward, Maggie Herold, Fumi Kosaka, Marisa Miller, Rachel Orr, and Katherine Rogers. I would also like to thank David Black, Joy Tutela, and Alix Reid for their friendship, assistance, and great ideas. My wife, Joann, and my children, Jenny and Colin, are always a source of inspiration, joy, and support. Without them, I could not do my work.

I especially thank April Prince for her devoted efforts and unique contributions. This book would not have been possible without her tireless work, imagination, and creativity.

CONTENTS

INTRODUCTION

★ ★ ★ ★ ★

A very smart, funny scientist once told a reporter that space isn't so far away. "It's only an hour's drive if your car could go straight up." He was right. That is how close we are to space.

But here's another way to think about space. The galaxies of outer space are filled with stars. Does ten billion trillion stars mean anything to you? It sounds like one of those phrases that little kids make up when they want to think of the absolutely hugest possible number there is. But that is how many stars astronomers say are out there in the universe. If everybody on Earth—all six billion people—counted 1,000 stars per second for twenty-four hours a day, it would take fifty years to count all those stars. You could get tired just thinking about it.

Of course our Sun, which gives light, energy, and life to Earth, is only one of those trillions of stars. Now space seems like a much bigger place, doesn't it?

Don't Know Much About® Space is meant to be an easy, interesting, and fun way to help you navigate around all that space. Just like a road map helps show the way to the beach, or a tour book tells you which sights to see when you visit a new city, this book introduces the sights and places that we know exist in our great big universe. It asks and answers a lot of questions you may have about space—and maybe a few you haven't thought of. It also asks some questions to which science has no answers yet!

As we continue to explore space, with exciting projects like the International Space Station, which was being put together a few hundred miles above Earth even as this book was being written, we'll answer some of those questions. But one thing is for certain: space will be part of our future. So it's a good idea to get to know the place where you and your children and grandchildren may someday explore and work—or just take a holiday. Happy space travels!

CHAPTER 1

WHO INVENTED ASTRONOMY?

VOICES OF THE UNIVERSE

66 Every cubic inch of space is a miracle. 99
—**Walt Whitman,** "Miracles," *Leaves of Grass*

Where does space begin?

Space begins where Earth's air ends. However, when astronauts go to space, they don't cross a borderline and pass a sign that says, "Welcome to outer space!" Earth's *atmosphere*—the layer of gases that surrounds our planet—just gets thinner and thinner the higher you are above the planet. At about 300 miles (480 km) above the surface, the lighter molecules in the air begin to escape Earth's gravity and drift into space. This region, about forty times higher than a jet can fly, is where space begins.

Where in space is Earth?

For thousands of years, people thought Earth was the center of the universe. After all, it certainly looks as though the Sun, planets, and stars revolve around us. But today we know that's far from the truth.

▲ A view of the Milky Way

Earth is just one planet out of nine that circle our Sun. The Sun is just one star in the billions of stars that make up our galaxy, the Milky Way. And the Milky Way is just one of hundreds of billions of *galaxies*, or groups of stars, in the universe.

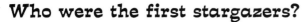

Who were the first stargazers?

People have been gazing at the stars ever since they could gaze at all (the people, not the stars). But the first civilization to actively study the stars and planets was probably that of the Babylonians. These people, who lived in Mesopotamia between the Tigris and Euphrates Rivers (present-day Iraq), created the first charts of the skies. Around 1580 B.C., for instance, they recorded on tablets the appearance and disappearance of the planet Venus, which they connected with the goddess Ishtar. The Egyptians and Chinese were also charting the stars by 1200 B.C. or so.

Over hundreds of years, these people noticed that there were patterns and predictable movements in the sky. As they watched the Sun, Moon, and stars move overhead, they realized they could use the heavens as a map, a calendar, and a clock. The skies directed ancient travelers and helped hunters and farmers know when to hunt seasonal animals and plant and harvest their crops.

Do we see the same sky the ancients did?

Yes. The sky we see today is almost identical to the sky seen by the first stargazers. What has changed is our view of that sky. Today air pollution and bright city lights can block our view of all but the brightest stars. Thousands of years ago, the stars blazed like a brilliant canopy overhead. (If you go stargazing at the top of a mountain or far away from the glare of city lights, you'll get a better idea of what the ancients saw.) It's no wonder astronomy became the first science—people studied the stars because they couldn't ignore them!

What were the first timekeeping devices?

They were calendars, and scientists have found some that may be more than 20,000 years old. These ancient "calendar sticks" were simple pieces of wood or bone scratched with marks to record the passing days and months. The first calendars used the 29 or 30 days between new moons as the twelve months that formed a year. (Can you see the connection between our English words *month* and *moon*?) But twelve lunar months are a few days short of a full year, so around 4200 B.C. the Egyptians created a calendar for a 365-day year based on the movement of the Sun.

Since people of early civilizations weren't rushing off to school or soccer practice, they didn't have much need for hours, minutes, and seconds. But they did notice that the shadows cast by the Sun changed throughout the day, shortening around noon and lengthening at the end of the day. They built tall pillars to make measuring and observing the shadows easier.

> **VOICES OF THE UNIVERSE**
>
> **❝** The Sun, Moon, and . . . planets were made for determining and preserving the numbers of time. **❞**
> —**Plato,** *Timaeus*

Why do we have an extra day every four years?

Just to make life interesting for everyone born on February 29. Actually, we have a 366-day *leap year* every four years because Earth's year (the time it takes Earth to circle the Sun) is actually 365 days, 5 hours, 48 minutes, and 45 seconds long. Those extra hours, minutes, and seconds add up to about one extra day every four years. Since it's only *about* one extra day, every 400 years three leap years are taken out to keep the calendar accurate.

Where is the Sun on Sunday?

In the sky—and in the word!

The original seven-day week started with the Babylonians, who believed seven was a lucky number. The Babylonians named the days of the week after their gods of the Sun, Moon, and planets. Later civilizations adopted this system, replacing the Babylonian names with the names of their own gods. Though you wouldn't recognize some of the names in English, can you guess which heavenly bodies inspired Monday and Saturday?

Who built perfectly placed pyramids for their pharaohs?

In the ages before modern science, many early cultures explained the workings of the universe as the will and actions of the gods. Some of the great structures built to honor these gods still stand today. Can you match these structures with the people who built them?

The builders of these tombs associated the pyramid shape with the Sun god Re and so adopted the shape for the resting places of their pharaohs (kings). Astronomers studied the stars to decide the best place to build a pyramid, then builders took precise measurements so the four sides aligned almost perfectly to north, south, east, and west. The alignment was thought to help the pharaoh's soul find its way to heaven.   *Egyptians*

These temples in Mexico and South America were the site of sacrifices (sometimes human sacrifices) to the gods. Their builders believed that the Sun needed blood to keep moving across the sky.   *Aztecs and Mayans*

Though the religious significance of the sacred stones at England's Stonehenge is unknown, the rocks are aligned with the Sun and Moon. Built between 1900 and 1600 B.C., the stones were probably placed to record important events in the sky. The rocks can be used to mark the summer and winter solstices (the longest and shortest days of the year) and the spring and autumnal equinoxes (when day and night are the same length).   *British priests*

Who invented astronomy?

The Greeks. Even though stars and planets had been mapped and charted by the Babylonians, Chinese, and Egyptians, astronomy actually became a *science* in Greece. About 550 B.C., a group of Greek philosophers began to move away from the mythology of the skies and see the universe in a new way. They liked the myth of the Sun god Helios (later called Apollo) pulling the Sun chariot across the sky well enough, but couldn't the universe, they said, be better understood through reason and observation?

About 200 years after these thinkers had begun trying to explain the order of the natural world, the great Greek philosopher Aristotle (384–322 B.C.) brought all their ideas together to form the first unified description of Earth and the heavens. Aristotle's thoughts would dominate philosophy and science for nearly 2,000 years.

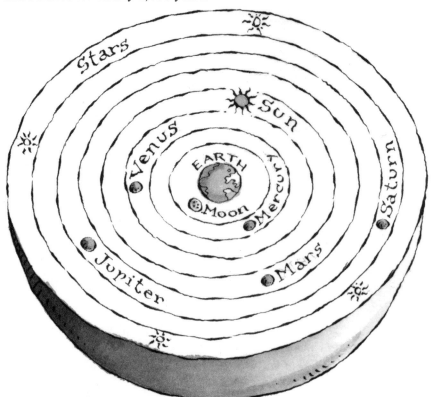

Aristotle said that Earth was the center of the universe. The Moon, Sun, planets, and stars moved in perfect circles around Earth, carried by clear shells of a transparent material like crystal. In fact, said Aristotle, there were fifty-five of these shells, each one nestled within the next, with Earth at the center. The heavens, which were perfect and unchanging, were kept in motion by a greater power, a "prime mover."

Aristotle was more a philosopher than a scientist. The first real astronomer was Hipparchus (c.146–127 B.C.), who created a catalog of 850 stars and their locations. Hipparchus introduced the practice of grouping the stars according to their *magnitude*, or brightness. He also discovered Earth's *precession*, which is the way Earth wobbles on its axis over the course of 26,000 years.

How many planets did the ancients know?

The five, besides Earth, that are visible to the naked eye: Mercury, Venus, Mars, Jupiter, and Saturn. These five planets, plus the Moon and stars, were the "seven heavens."

What does astronomy have to do with astrology?

Nothing, really. *Astronomy* is the science of studying everything in the universe beyond Earth's atmosphere. *Astrology* is the belief that people's lives are affected by the movement of the stars and planets.

As the early stargazers began to see the order and pattern of the heavens, they decided that this universal order must be seen on Earth, as well. Astrologers created complicated charts that showed which stars, planets, and constellations (star pictures) were overhead at any moment. The planets and constellations that were overhead at a baby's birth, for instance, were said to influence his or her life and personality.

Some people today still believe in astrology, or at least enjoy reading predictions in horoscopes, which are forecasts of the future based on the position of stars and planets. However, astrology is not a science, and astronomers do not appreciate being confused with astrologers.

Did Aristotle know the world was round?

He did. Though some people think that Christopher Columbus's voyage in 1492 was the first evidence that the world was round, in reality Aristotle had realized this nearly 2,000 years before. Aristotle wrote that during a total lunar eclipse, when our planet comes between the Sun and the Moon, Earth casts a curved shadow on the Moon. Earth would have to be spherical, like a ball, to do that. Aristotle also said that when a person traveled north or south, new stars came into view that couldn't be seen before. If the world were flat, there wouldn't be anyplace for stars to "hide" like that.

Who thought Earth was the center of the universe?

Just about everybody on the planet, until about 400 years ago. If Earth moved, people said, we'd all certainly know it. Birds wouldn't be able to fly against the wind as Earth sailed through the air. Falling leaves would all scatter in one direction. If you threw a ball straight up, it would come down somewhere else. Anyway, the great philosophers said that our planet was the unmoving center of creation.

Five hundred years after Aristotle, the Greek astronomer Ptolemy reinforced this *geocentric*, or Earth-centered (*geo* means "earth"), view of the universe. In the second century A.D., Ptolemy wrote a book that pulled together everything known about the heavens so far, and added to it. The book, later named the *Almagest*, or the "greatest," by the Arabs, became the basis of astronomy for nearly 1,500 years. Its contents, which became known as the Ptolemaic system, were adopted by the Roman Catholic Church—largely because of the idea that the heavens were perfect and controlled by a "prime mover" (or God).

> **VOICES OF THE UNIVERSE**
>
> 66 Mortal as I am, I know that I am born for a day, but when I follow the serried multitude of the stars in their circular course, my feet no longer touch the earth; I ascend to Zeus himself to feast me on ambrosia, the food of the gods. 99
>
> —Claudius Ptolemaeus

Claudius Ptolemaeus (c. A.D. 100–178)

Claudius Ptolemaeus, known as Ptolemy, was a Greek-Egyptian astronomer, geographer, and mathematician. Ptolemy's many good ideas and observations about the world were, unfortunately, offset by some significant bad ones. For instance, Ptolemy calculated that Earth was about one-fourth smaller than it really is. This in turn led Christopher Columbus to think that a trip west to reach Asia would be much shorter than it actually was. Had he known the real size of the world, Columbus might never have sailed, and history might be much different.

Still, Ptolemy did more things right than he did wrong. He took the fields of geography, astronomy, optics, and other areas of knowledge and organized them into scientific systems, provable by mathematics. His work set the standard for these sciences for more than a thousand years.

Who turned the Ptolemaic system on its head?

It didn't happen all at once, but a new view of the universe started to spread when Polish astronomer Nicolaus Copernicus (1473–1543) said Ptolemy might be wrong. Copernicus was the first person, except for a few early Greeks such as Aristarchus, to suggest that Earth and all the other planets move around the Sun. After looking at and taking measurements of the skies for thirty years, Copernicus thought a *heliocentric*, or Sun-centered view of the universe (*helios* means "Sun") made more sense than an Earth-centered one. A Sun-centered system was much simpler; the orbits of the planets could be explained more easily.

Copernicus knew that his Sun-centered idea could get him in big trouble with religious leaders of the time, who favored an Earth-centered view of the universe. So Copernicus delayed publishing his book, *On the Revolutions of the Heavenly Spheres*, until he was literally on his deathbed. But Copernicus needn't have worried about offending anyone, since church leaders dismissed the book by saying it was just an exercise in math, not a real proposal of how the universe might work. It was true that Copernicus couldn't prove his idea. That would be left to another astronomer, and the telescope.

VOICES OF THE UNIVERSE

66 Finally we shall place the Sun himself at the center of the universe. All this is suggested by the systematic procession of events and the harmony of the whole universe if only we face the facts, as they say, 'with both eyes open.' 99

—**Nicolaus Copernicus**, *On the Revolutions of the Heavenly Spheres*

What did astronomer Tycho Brahe do to Aristotle's crystal spheres?

He smashed them to pieces. Copernicus wasn't the only one who saw that the ancients' views of the universe didn't completely make sense. Dutch astronomer Tycho Brahe observed things in the sky that also contradicted Aristotle's idea of an unchanging cosmos held up by crystal spheres.

In 1572, Brahe studied what appeared to be a new star in the sky. (One story says that Brahe was so amazed at the sight that he asked a neighbor to hit him to prove he wasn't dreaming.) In truth, what Brahe saw was a *supernova*, or the bright explosion of an old star. This disproved Aristotle's theory that nothing among the stars ever changed. In 1577, Brahe also observed a comet streaming across the sky. From his observations, Brahe concluded that either the comet had come crashing through one of Aristotle's crystal spheres, or the spheres did not exist at all.

Brahe challenged Aristotle, but he didn't go so far as to support the Copernican view of the universe. Instead, Brahe proposed a compromise: he said that all the planets revolved around the Sun, which revolved around Earth. Not many people followed this confusing theory.

COSMIC SUPERSTARS:

Tycho Brahe (1546–1601)

Tycho Brahe was an unusual character. He was born in Denmark but was kidnapped and raised by his uncle in Germany. He studied math and astronomy and was so passionate about them that he lost most of his nose in a midnight duel with another student. (They argued about which of them was a better mathematician.) For the rest of his life, Brahe had to wear a fake nose made of gold, silver, and wax.

It's a good thing astronomers don't depend on their sense of smell. They do depend on their eyesight, and Brahe's was extraordinary. He was the best naked-eye astronomer who ever lived. Over the course of twenty years, Brahe mapped 1,000 stars with incredible precision. Brahe used his observations to create his own set of astronomical records, which was unusual in a day when most astronomers worked from charts that were hundreds of years old.

Who invented the telescope?

Though he probably wasn't the first to do it, Dutch eyeglass maker Hans Lippershey gets credit for putting two lenses on either end of a tube in 1608 and creating a "spyglass." (Even then, it wasn't Lippershey but his children who discovered that the double lenses made a nearby weathervane look bigger.) These early instruments were not much more than toys because their lenses weren't very strong.

The first person to turn a spyglass toward the sky was an Italian mathematician and professor named Galileo Galilei (1564–1642). Galileo, who heard about the Dutch spyglass and began making his own, realized right away how useful the device could be to armies and sailors. As he made better and better telescopes (as they were later named) Galileo decided to point one at the Moon. Our view of the universe would never be the same.

How do telescopes work to make things look bigger?

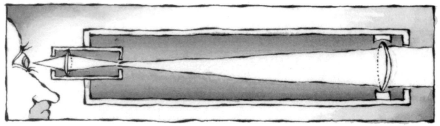

▲ Refracting telescope

Telescopes basically give you bigger eyes. The reason you see is that light enters your pupils, or the small black centers of your eyes. The more light that enters your pupils, the brighter objects will appear. You might have noticed that your pupils grow larger when you go into a dark area. They do that to let in more light. But your pupils can only get so big (about as wide as a pea). Telescopes "cheat" by gathering light from a much larger area and focusing it into a beam that can fit through your pupil. That makes faraway objects look brighter, larger, and clearer.

VOICES OF THE UNIVERSE

❝O, telescope, instrument of much knowledge, more precious than any sceptre, is not he who holds thee in his hand made king and lord of the works of God?❞

—**Johannes Kepler,** *Diopterice*

Why was Galileo arrested?

Galileo was arrested by the Roman Catholic Church because the church leaders didn't like what he saw with his new telescope. Galileo had found that the heavenly bodies were not the perfect spheres described by Aristotle. He discovered that the Moon wasn't smooth but had mountains and valleys like Earth. He also discovered spots on the Sun, rings around Saturn, and four moons around Jupiter. Even lovely Venus was changeable, going through phases, like the Moon, from crescent to full.

Not only could he see that the heavens weren't perfect, Galileo could tell from his observations that Copernicus was right—Earth and other planets did revolve around the Sun. Galileo published his findings in 1610 in a small book called *The Starry Messenger*.

The church warned Galileo to stop spreading Copernicus's ideas, but Galileo went ahead and wrote another book about them anyway. When Galileo's new book, *Dialogue Concerning the Two Chief World Systems*, came out, he was convicted of *heresy*, or going against church beliefs, and sentenced to house arrest. (That's like being in jail, except it's your house you can't leave.) His *Dialogue* was placed on the church's *Index*, a list of forbidden books.

A few years before Galileo looked through his first telescope, a stubborn Italian priest named Giordano Bruno got in trouble for promoting a Sun-centered universe. Going even farther than Galileo in his theories, he claimed that the universe was infinite, containing many worlds just like our own. Bruno's views greatly angered the church. He was asked to take them back on pain of death, and refused. In 1600, Bruno was burned to death by the church.

COSMIC SUPERSTARS:

Galileo Galilei (1564–1642)

Galileo was one of the first scientists to use what we call the *scientific method*. He would make a guess about something and then do test after test to see if he was right. Aristotle and Ptolemy had used logic and reasoning more than measurement, so they had very little proof, if any, to back up their views. Galileo wanted evidence.

Galileo struggled with religious and scientific beliefs that seemed to contradict each other. Before he was sentenced to house arrest, the court asked him if he wanted to take back what he'd written—especially his claim that Earth moved around the Sun. Knowing what had happened to Bruno and others, Galileo ultimately did take it back. Legend says that as Galileo left the courtroom, he muttered under his breath, *"E pur si muove."* ("Nevertheless, it moves.") Though he always knew what he believed, it's quite unlikely that he actually said this, considering what would've become of him had anyone heard it!

66 Philosophy is written in this grand book—I mean the universe—which stands continually open to our gaze, but it cannot be understood unless one first learns to comprehend the language and interpret the characters in which it is written. It is written in the language of mathematics, and its characters are triangles, circles, and other geometrical figures, without which it is humanly impossible to understand a single word of it; without these, one is wandering about in a dark labyrinth. **99**

— **Galileo Galilei,** *Il Saggiatore*

The Catholic Church didn't acknowledge that Earth moved around the Sun for hundreds of years. Galileo was pardoned (forgiven of his crimes) in 1992, 350 years after his death. That seems incredible. But in some ways, we all ignore that it's Earth, and not the Sun, that moves—like when we talk about the Sun "rising" and "setting"!

COSMIC SUPERSTARS:

Johannes Kepler (1571–1630)

German mathematician Johannes Kepler had worked as Tycho Brahe's assistant. When Brahe died, he left his records of his observations to Kepler, with instructions to use them to disprove Copernican theory. So it's funny that after years of studying the records and the motion of the planets, Kepler knew that Copernicus's theory of a Sun-centered system is true. He urged Galileo to publish his research and help prove that Earth and other planets move around the Sun.

So if the planets don't circle Earth within crystal spheres, how do they travel?

In a way, the planets travel in a sort of racetrack around the Sun. They don't travel on actual tracks, but each does have a special path, or *orbit*. Johannes Kepler discovered that the orbits, instead of being perfectly round as had been thought for 1,600 years, were actually *elliptical*, or shaped like a stretched-out circle. This was a controversial view just as Galileo's was, since the heavenly bodies were supposed to travel in perfect circles, the circle being the "perfect form."

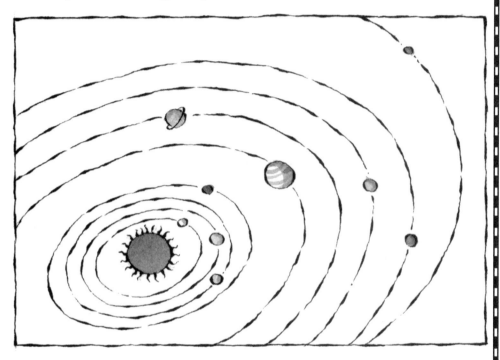

Kepler also discovered that the planets travel at different speeds at different points in their orbits (closer to the Sun, they travel faster), and that the planets farthest away from the Sun take the longest to travel around it. Earth's travel time around the Sun, or its year, is 365.24 days. But years on the other planets range from Mercury's 88 (Earth) days to Pluto's 248 (Earth) years! If the solar system is a racetrack, it's not a very exciting one, because Mercury, the closest planet to the Sun, always wins the race.

What did an apple teach us about the universe?

English scientist Isaac Newton said that after watching an apple fall from a tree in 1666, he had a powerful realization about *gravity*—the force that pulls all objects toward each other. People had known about gravity on Earth for a long time. (It didn't take much to notice that things

> If you tie a string around a ball and spin it around in a circle, the pull you feel on the string is like the pull of gravity that keeps the Moon circling around the Earth.

always fall down, not up or sideways.) But Newton was the first to show that the force that pulled the apple to the ground, or toward the center of Earth, was the same force that kept our Moon traveling around Earth and the planets traveling around the Sun. Newton said that if the Moon had its way, it would travel in a straight line through the universe. However, since the Moon is captured by Earth's gravity, it's also pulled to the center of Earth. The force that keeps the Moon moving outward balances the force that pulls it toward Earth, so it moves in a loop around the planet.

Whether Newton was pulling our leg with his apple story, we'll never know. He'd been thinking about the motion of the Moon and planets long before he saw the falling piece of fruit, so he certainly didn't figure out gravity in the time it took for an apple to drop from a tree. Newton told his biographer that the event brought the theory of gravity together in his mind.

COSMIC SUPERSTARS:

Isaac Newton (1642–1727)

Isaac Newton was a brilliant scientist who made many contributions to physics, math, and astronomy: He discovered the nature of light and the laws of universal gravitation. He invented calculus, a kind of math used to make complex calculations. He improved Galileo's telescope by using mirrors instead of lenses. On top of all that, he served in the British Parliament and was appointed Master of the Royal Mint. In 1705, Newton became Sir Isaac Newton, the first scientist ever to be knighted.

No one is sure where the boy from a small town in England got his smarts—his father, who died before Isaac was born, didn't know how to write and signed his will with an *X*. Newton would become so involved in his studies and teaching at Cambridge University in England that he often forgot to change his clothes, comb his hair, and eat his meals. Newton said that his work was built on that of great scientists, astronomers, and philosophers before him, including Copernicus, Kepler, and Galileo. When someone asked an elderly Newton how he'd done it all, he said, "If I have seen further, it is by standing on the shoulders of giants."

How much do you weigh?

That depends on what and how much you eat, how much you exercise, and what genes you inherit from your parents—in a word, your *mass*: how much matter is in your body. Mass means all the matter in an object—all its atoms together.

Your weight really depends on two masses: yours, and the planet's. Gravity is the attraction of two masses for each other. The larger the masses, and the closer they are to each other, the stronger the force of gravity. What you feel as weight on Earth is gravity pulling your mass toward Earth's mass.

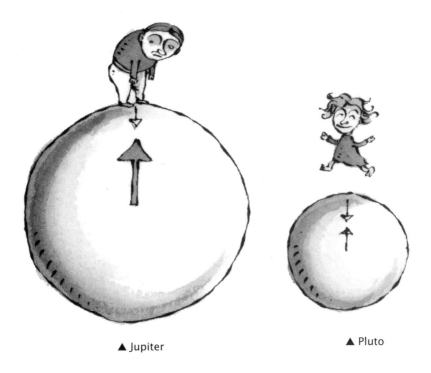

▲ Jupiter

▲ Pluto

Each planet has a different mass, and therefore a different amount of gravity. The bigger the planet, the more gravity it usually has. So if you were on tiny Pluto, you'd bounce all over the place because you'd weigh much less than you do on Earth. If you could stand on gigantic Jupiter, you'd be so heavy you could hardly walk. Your weight would be different in those places, but your mass would be the same.

If you weigh 100 pounds on Earth, here's what you'd weigh on other bodies in space:

Mercury	40 lbs (18 kg)	**Saturn**	110 lbs (50 kg)
Venus	90 lbs (41 kg)	**Uranus**	90 lbs (41 kg)
Moon	17 lbs (7 kg)	**Neptune**	110 lbs (50 kg)
Mars	40 lbs (18 kg)	**Pluto**	7 lbs (3 kg)
Jupiter	249 lbs (113 kg)	**The Sun**	2,800 lbs (1,270 kg)

If Earth is round, why don't people on the other side of the world fall off?

Good question! Gravity pulls everything toward the center of a mass. That means everyone on a planet is pulled toward the planet's center, so nothing flies off into space. Gravity is also what holds the planets in their orbits around the Sun. The center of mass in the solar system is just outside the Sun's surface.

Why were Newton's ideas accepted and Galileo's rejected?

Both Newton and Galileo lived in a time called the *Renaissance*, which means "rebirth." The Renaissance was a period of great change in Europe that transformed how people lived, learned, and thought.

In medieval times, the Catholic Church had dominated education and the arts. But in the 1350s, Italians began to rediscover works of the ancient Greeks and Romans that focused on independent thought and on doing experiments to test theories. Ideas spread more quickly as trade and cities grew and as the printing press came into use. People became eager for new ideas, especially scientific ones. By the time Isaac Newton arrived on the scene—he was born the year Galileo died—people were more receptive to new ideas about the universe and their place in it.

WHY DOES THE SUN SHINE?

The Solar System

Is the solar system as old as the universe?

Nope. Our Sun and planets are only middle aged compared to the universe. Five billion years ago, the solar system was a huge, cold, spinning cloud of dust and gas. Something—maybe a shock wave from a nearby exploding star—started the gas cloud compressing, or pulling in on itself. As gravity pulled the dust and gas closer together, the cloud began to spin faster and faster and to heat up. It spun into a flat disk like pizza dough, with most of the matter gathered into a hot lump at the disk's center. As gravity pulled that central lump together, it got hotter and hotter. Finally, about 4.5 billion years ago, a process called *nuclear fusion* (see p. 133) started up inside that central mass, and the Sun was born.

Scientists think the bodies in our solar system were made of leftover matter (gas and dust) from when the Sun was born. The four planets closest to the Sun are called the *rocky planets* because—you guessed it—they're small, hard, and rocky. The next four planets are called the *gas giants* because they're much larger and mostly made of liquid and gases. Tiny Pluto, the last planet we know of, is a bit of an oddball: a mixture of rock and ice on the outer fringes of the solar system.

Who are Earth's neighbors in the solar system?

The solar system includes anything orbiting the Sun. Our solar system is home to nine *planets*, or large objects that travel around a star. Most planets have one or more *moons*, or smaller bodies of rock or ice that orbit them. So far, we've discovered 72 moons in our solar system. The solar system also includes lopsided miniplanets called *asteroids*; balls of ice and dust called *comets*; and small floating space rocks, pieces of comets or asteroids, called *meteoroids*. Each planet, moon, asteroid, comet, and meteoroid travels around the Sun in its own orbit.

To remember the order of the planets from the Sun outward, all you have to do is remember this sentence: My Very Eager Mother Just Sent Us Nine Pizzas. Each first letter is the first letter of one of the planets: Mercury, Venus, Earth, Mars, Jupiter, Saturn, Uranus, Neptune, Pluto.

THE SUN

Size:	870,000 miles (1,400,000 km) across
Age:	4.5 billion years
Surface temperature:	10,000 °F (5,500 °C)
Core temperature:	29 million °F (16 million °C)

Why does the Sun look different from all the other stars in the sky?

The Sun is an ordinary, medium-sized star that's much like countless others. It looks different because it's so close to Earth—just a measly 93 million miles (150 million km) away. That might not seem very close, but it is when you consider that the next closest star to us is 25 trillion miles (42 trillion km) away! That's more than 100,000 times farther than our sun.

Is the Sun the biggest star in our galaxy?

The Sun isn't the biggest or brightest star in our galaxy, but it is, by far, the largest body in the solar system. It contains a whopping 99.86 percent of the solar system's mass. The planets are so tiny in comparison that 1.3 *million* Earths could fit inside the Sun. Put another way, if the Sun were the size of a soccer ball, the Earth would be about half the size of a pea!

> **WARNING!**
>
> CAUTION! You should never look directly at the Sun. Don't even look at it through sunglasses or film. It's so bright that it could blind you for the rest of your life. The great astronomer Galileo had severe eye damage, probably from looking at the Sun.

Why does the Sun shine?

Because if it didn't, we wouldn't get up in the morning. Actually, the Sun, like other stars, shines because it's an intensely hot, bubbling ball of gas. It glows like the heated coils of an electric stove. But the Sun doesn't burn like a stove or a bonfire; if it did, it would have burned out long ago.

Instead, the Sun is more like a gigantic hydrogen bomb, creating light and heat by turning hydrogen gas into helium gas. This happens under super-

Unlike the solid layers of Earth, the layers of the Sun are made of swirling gases. Its surface looks like boiling tomato soup.

high temperatures at the Sun's *core*, or center. The Sun's core can get as hot as 29 million °F (16 million °C)!

Surrounding its core, the Sun has cooler layers called the *radiative zone*, *convection zone*, and the Sun's outer layer, the *photosphere*, where the Sun's atmosphere begins. Above the photosphere things start getting warmer again in the Sun's *chromosphere*. At the edge of the chromosphere is the *corona*, the outer layer of the atmosphere that's about 1.8 million °F (1 million °C).

Will the Sun ever stop shining?

Yes. Like all stars, the Sun will stop shining one day. But don't worry—that won't be for a long, long time. The Sun will burn the way it does today for about another 5 billion years. Then it will run out of hydrogen fuel and start to cool and brighten. In the process, it will get so big that it will swallow up Mercury and Venus and turn Earth to a bubbling, boiling mass.

The inside of the Sun is so tightly packed with particles bumping into each other that it takes a million years for light to make its way to the surface from the core. But from there it only takes eight minutes to travel through space and reach Earth.

Does the Sun have freckles?

In a way. Though the Sun looks smooth and solid from Earth, its boiling surface has frecklelike *sunspots*, or dark areas that are cooler than the rest of the Sun. Sunspots are areas where magnetic activity is especially strong and heat has a harder time flowing to the surface. Sunspots, which can be ten or more times the size of Earth, usually appear in pairs or groups and last a few days or weeks. The number of spots goes up and down in a regular cycle that lasts eleven years. At minimum, the Sun may show no spots at all; at maximum, it may have more than 100 at a time.

When is it like nighttime in the middle of the day?

During a solar *eclipse*. A solar eclipse happens when the Moon comes between the earth and the Sun and blocks the Sun's light. (If you shine a flashlight in a dark room and then put your hand right in front of it, you'll get an idea of what's happening during an eclipse.)

About twice a year, a *partial eclipse* happens when the Moon blocks just some of the Sun's rays. About seventy times in every 100 years, the Moon blocks out all the Sun's light in a *total eclipse*. That's when the real drama takes place. During a total eclipse, the Moon slips across the face of the Sun like the lens cap on a camera. The sky grows dark. The air cools. The brightest stars come out. All that can be seen of the Sun is its corona, the faint outer layer that stretches for millions of miles into space.

▲ In this photograph the Sun's light is blocked and then reappears as the Moon moves from right to left.

How can the tiny Moon cover the gigantic Sun?

It does it just by chance. The Moon looks as big as the Sun because it's closer to our eyes. The Sun is about four hundred times wider across than the Moon, but it also happens to be about four hundred times farther away. On no other planet does this condition exist.

To see what's happening, try this: Close one eye, and hold your thumb in front of the other, open eye. Place your thumb in front of something big in the distance, like a car. Move your thumb toward and away from you. If your thumb is close to your face, it will cover up the entire car. If it's farther away, it will only cover some of the car.

UNIVERSAL LANGUAGE

The word **eclipse** comes from the Greek word for "abandonment," because it looked to the Greeks like the Sun was abandoning Earth.

How can you watch an eclipse safely?

Remember that you can go blind from looking directly at the Sun! If you want to watch a solar eclipse, you have to use a special tool so you don't hurt your eyes.

To make a simple eclipse viewer, you'll need:

scissors

aluminum foil

a pin

two pieces of cardboard, at least one of them white (so you can project a picture of the Sun onto it, like a movie screen)

1. Cut a small square out of the middle of the nonwhite piece of cardboard.

2. Cover the square with aluminum foil.

3. Make a pinhole in the middle of the foil. You're ready for the eclipse!

During the eclipse, with the Sun behind you, hold the pinhole cardboard in your hands and put the white cardboard on the ground in front of you. Sunlight passing through the hole will project a tiny image of the Sun and its eclipse on the white cardboard. The farther you are from the white cardboard, the bigger the image of the eclipse will be. Make sure you're ready, because most eclipses last only two or three minutes.

UNIVERSAL LANGUAGE

Though it sounds more like the sound you make when you sneeze, **syzygy** (SIH-zih-gee) is the term for when three bodies in space are lined up in a row. During an eclipse, the Sun, Moon, and Earth are in syzygy.

MERCURY

Size: 3,031 miles (4,878 km) across

Length of day: 176 Earth days

Length of year: 88 Earth days

Average distance from Sun: 36 million miles
  (58 million km)

Average surface temperature: -300 °F to 800 °F
  (-184 °C to 427 °C)

Number of known moons: 0

Number of known rings: 0

Weight of a 100-pound Earthling: 40 pounds (18 kg)

Why is Mercury so hard to see from Earth?

Partly because it's so small that you need a telescope, and partly because it
hides out in the Sun's glare. You can't see Mercury at night, because it
never travels very far from the Sun. (When the Sun sets, Mercury soon
follows.) It's dangerous to look for Mercury during the day, because you
can end up staring at the Sun. The best times to spy little Mercury are just
before sunrise or just after sunset.

Why would mice like Mercury?

Because Mercury looks like a ball of gray Swiss cheese. It's covered with
craters, or round, shallow holes where asteroids and meteoroids have hit
the surface. Some of Mercury's craters are hundreds of miles wide. There
are even craters within craters! The craters hang around because Mercury
has barely any air, and no rain, to wear them away.

Does Beethoven live on Mercury?

Yes. But on Mercury, Beethoven isn't a musician. Instead, it's a large crater
named after the famous composer. Some of Mercury's other features are
also named for famous people, like Shakespeare and Michelangelo.
However, the largest feature on Mercury is the Caloris ("Hot") Basin, a
bowl-like crater the size of Texas. The basin is surrounded by mountains
that make it look like a giant bull's-eye.

Nearly everything we know about Mercury's surface comes from close-up pictures taken by the *Mariner 10* spacecraft that flew past the planet in 1974 and 1975.

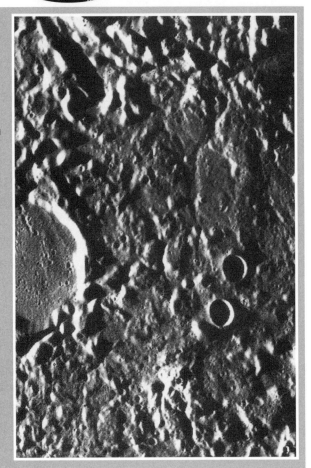

 ## On Mercury, a day is longer than a year.

True. Since Mercury is the closest planet to the Sun, it has the shortest distance to travel around it. Mercury revolves around the Sun in only 88 Earth days, giving it the shortest year in the solar system. No wonder Mercury was named for the speedy Roman messenger of the gods!

But Mercury takes its own sweet time—176 Earth days—to rotate around just once. That makes its day twice as long as its year. If you think that would make birthdays confusing, don't worry. Humans could never survive in Mercury's extreme temperatures. In the long daytime, it's a whopping 800 °F (427 °C). During the long night, the temperature drops more than 1,000 degrees, to about -300 °F (-184 °C).

VENUS

Size: 7,520 miles (12,100 km) across

Length of day: 243 Earth days

Length of year: 225 Earth days

Distance from Sun: 67 million miles (108 million km)

Average surface temperature: about 900 °F (480 °C)

Number of known moons: 0

Number of known rings: 0

Weight of a 100-pound Earthling: 90 pounds (41 kg)

If Venus is a planet, why is it called the "morning and evening star"?

Because Venus shines in our skies like a star for a few hours after sunset and a few hours before sunrise. The Romans thought the planet was so gorgeous that they named it after their goddess of love and beauty.

Venus is so bright that it's often mistaken for a UFO. It shines brilliantly because it's covered with thick clouds that reflect the Sun's light. For many years, scientists thought that under those clouds Venus might be a lot like home. Venus was actually nicknamed our "sister planet" because it's our closest planetary neighbor and it's almost the same size as Earth. However, we've learned that very little about Venus, except its size, is anything like Earth.

If it's always cloudy on Venus, why is it so hot there?

Venus's thick atmosphere, made mostly of carbon dioxide, gives the planet a stifling average temperature of 900 °F (480 °C). That's hot enough to melt lead! The carbon dioxide traps the Sun's heat, which gets in but can't get out. This is called the *greenhouse effect* because the glass windows in a garden greenhouse do the same thing. But don't let the word *greenhouse* mislead you. There are no plants, and there is no life, on Venus. Venus is the hottest planet in the solar system. It's even hotter than Mercury, which is right next door to the Sun.

Venus's clouds aren't made of water vapor, like Earth's. Instead, they're made of poisonous sulfuric acid.

Does Venus have a crush on you?

Venus—its atmosphere, anyway—has a crush on everything. The planet's air is so thick that it presses down ninety-eight times as hard as Earth's atmosphere. That's as much pressure as you would feel 3,000 feet (914 m) underwater. If you stood without protection on Venus's surface, you'd be crushed and roasted before you could breathe in too many of its poisonous fumes.

How can we map the surface of Venus if we can't see through the planet's thick clouds?

We wouldn't want to send astronauts through the clouds into that dangerous place. So instead we sent a space probe named *Magellan*. *Probes* are spacecraft that are programmed to do experiments but don't

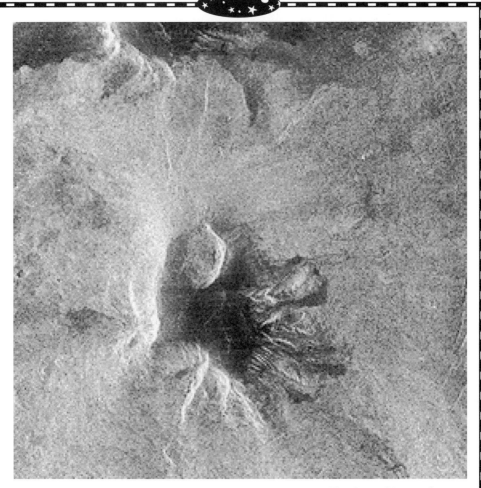

▲ The Sapas Mons volcano

carry people. In 1990, *Magellan* used high-powered radar to bounce microwaves off the surface of Venus. By measuring the time it took for the microwaves to travel to the surface and back, scientists were able to make a model of the planet's surface. A few probes have also plunged through the clouds and withstood the intense heat and air pressure long enough to send a few pictures back to Earth. The pictures showed a mostly flat landscape with few craters, though the planet does have many volcanoes.

Like Mercury, Venus's day is longer than its year. The unique thing about Venus is that it rotates backward compared to the other planets. On Venus, the Sun rises in the west. No one knows why this is so.

EARTH

Size: 7,926 miles across (12,755 km)

Length of day: 23 hours, 56 minutes

Length of year: 365.24 Earth days

Distance from Sun: 93 million miles (150 million km)

Average surface temperature: 59 °F (15 °C)

Number of known moons: 1

Number of known rings: 0

Weight of a 100-pound Earthling: 100 pounds (45 kg)

What's so special about Earth?

Earth is the only planet where we know there is life. Earth's distance from the Sun gives it just the right temperature to keep water in its three forms—liquid, ice, and vapor. Earth's atmosphere provides oxygen to breathe, protects us from the Sun's dangerous rays, and keeps our planet warm.

What's between Earth and space?

There are five layers of atmosphere between Earth and space. We live in the *troposphere*, which extends about 6 to 10 miles (10 to 16 km) above Earth. We can live in the troposphere unprotected, but that gets harder and harder the farther you get from the ground. If you've ever been to the top of a mountain, you know it's harder to breathe up there because the air is thinner and there's less oxygen. There's also less protection from the Sun's harmful ultraviolet, or UV, rays, so you have to be careful to slather on extra sunblock. Most of our weather happens in the troposphere.

Jet airplanes fly in the next layer, called the *stratosphere*. That's where you'll find the famous ozone layer that screens out the Sun's UV rays. Then comes the *mesosphere*, where the air is still thick enough to burn up meteorites. Space shuttles circle around Earth in the *thermosphere*, but that's still not quite space. Space travelers must go past the outermost layer of the atmosphere, the *exosphere*.

Atmospheric layer	Distance above Earth	Travelers
Exosphere	400+ miles (644+ km)	satellites
Thermosphere	50–400 miles (80–644 km)	space shuttles, auroras
Mesosphere	30–50 miles (48–80 km)	flaming meteorites
Stratosphere	10–30 miles (16–48 km)	airplanes, weather balloons, clouds
Troposphere	6–10 miles (10–16 km)	humans, helicopters, weather, clouds

Why doesn't Earth have craters, like the Moon?

It does—about 200 of them. The most famous may be Meteor Crater, in the Arizona desert. That crater formed about 50 thousand years ago when a meteoroid collided with Earth. The hole is almost 600 feet (183 m) deep and a mile (1.6 km) wide. You can climb down to the bottom. Scientists have also found evidence of a huge crater, 121 miles (195 km) wide, under Mexico's Yucatán Peninsula. Many people believe that an asteroid might

Earth is named for the old English word for ground or soil. But only about 30 percent of our planet's surface is actually land—the rest is water. Earth got its nickname, the "Blue Planet," because it looks blue from outer space.

have crashed into Earth there 65 million years ago, kicking up dust that changed Earth's climate and led to the extinction of the dinosaurs.

Earth has actually been hit by more space rocks than the Moon has, since Earth is bigger. But our weather and the movement of Earth's crust have worn most of the craters smooth. The airless Moon doesn't have weather or moving crust, so many of its oldest craters are still there.

Then why isn't the whole Earth nice and smooth?

With all the wind and rain wearing down Earth's surface, you'd think it would be as smooth as a bowling ball. However, Earth's surface is divided into huge plates that are constantly moving. You don't usually feel the movement, except when there's an earthquake, but where these plates crunch into each other or move apart, mountains and valleys form. Hot, semimelted rock from inside our planet also wells out onto the surface, creating volcanic peaks.

How long have humans been around?

Human existence amounts to the blink of an eye in the history of the universe. If that history were a twenty-four-hour day, Earth wouldn't exist until just before dinnertime, and humans would arrive during the last two seconds! But Earth is home to an amazing variety of plants, animals, and other life-forms, from enormous elephants and redwood trees to tiny insects and bacteria. Most of those life-forms have been around much longer than we have.

This timeline shows when the universe, Earth, and its life-forms began:

15 billion years ago	Universe forms
4.6 billion years ago	The Sun, Earth, Moon, and solar system form
3.5 billion years ago	Microbes (living things so small you can't see them without a microscope) form
600 million years ago	Shelled sea animals form
350 million years ago	Plants thrive
350 million years ago	Amphibians (cold-blooded animals that can live in both water and on land) develop
300 million years ago	Age of the reptiles (scaly, cold-blooded animals) begins
200 million years ago	Oxygen in atmosphere reaches current levels
110 million years ago	Dinosaurs rule Earth; modern continents begin to form
65 million years ago	Dinosaurs die out
2 million years ago	Early humans appear
30,000 years ago	Modern humans appear
1969	Humans walk on the Moon

THE MOON

Size: 2,160 miles across (3,476 km)

Length of day: about 29 Earth days

Length of year: 1 Earth year

Distance from Earth: 238,000 miles

Average surface temperature: -260 °F (-127 °C) to 240 °F (116 °C)

Weight of a 100-pound Earthling: 17 pounds (7 kg)

Was the Moon ever part of Earth?

Maybe. Some scientists think that the Moon was a part of Earth that broke off in a collision with a planet-sized rock long ago. Other scientists think that our Moon and other moons in the solar system might have formed at the same time as the planets. They might also be bodies captured by a planet's gravity.

 ## The Moon never turns its back on us.

True. The same side of the Moon always faces us. That's because the amount of time it takes the Moon to rotate once, relative to the stars, just happens to be exactly the same amount of time it takes the Moon to travel around Earth.

Why isn't the Moon like any other body in the universe?

Because it's the only body in the universe that humans have ever visited. No one has been there since 1972, but it's likely that astronauts will return in the early part of this century to begin building a station or colony on the Moon.

How does the Moon make its light?

It doesn't. Stars are the only bodies in space that make their own light. The Moon is a big ball of rock that can't shine by itself. Instead, it reflects light from the Sun the same way a mirror does. Planets also reflect the Sun's light in this way.

The water in Earth's oceans chases the Moon.

True! If you've been to the ocean, you might have noticed that the water level rises and falls about every twelve hours. This happens because the Moon (and Sun's) gravity pulls on the water and on Earth. When the Moon is overhead, the water underneath rises to meet it. Even Earth's center moves toward the Moon, pulling away from the ocean on its far side. This means there are two *high tides* happening simultaneously: one in the ocean facing the Moon, and the other in the ocean on the opposite side of Earth. *Low tide* happens at the same time midway between these two points. The movement of the Moon keeps the oceans in constant transition between high and low tides.

Why is the Moon different shapes on different nights?

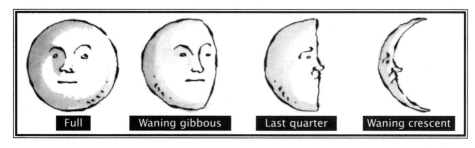

The Moon is like a magician: it doesn't actually change shape; it just looks like it does. That's because we can see only the part of the Moon that's lit by the Sun. As the Moon revolves around Earth, the amount of the sunlit side we can see changes. When we can see the whole, round Moon, we say it's a *full moon*. When we can see only one part of the sunlit side, we call it either *gibbous*, a *quarter moon*, or, when it is a sliver, a *crescent*. And when the Sun shines on the side of the Moon that's facing away from us, we can't see the Moon at all. This is called a *new moon*. When the Moon looks like it's getting bigger, we say it's *waxing*. When the Moon seems to be growing smaller, we say it's *waning*.

Many Native American cultures gave names to the full moons of the year. The names reflect what's happening at that time of year. Some of the most common names are:

January	Old Moon	**July**	Thunder or Hay Moon
February	Hunger, Snow, or Wolf Moon	**August**	Green Corn or Hay Moon
March	Sap or Crow Moon	**September**	Fruit or Harvest Moon
April	Grass or Egg Moon	**October**	Hunter's Moon
May	Planting or Milk Moon	**November**	Frosty or Beaver Moon
June	Rose, Flower, or Strawberry Moon	**December**	Long Night Moon

UNIVERSAL LANGUAGE

The light of a full moon has long been associated with evil and disaster. The word **lunatic** comes from the Latin name for the Moon, **luna,** because people believed that the rays of the Moon when full caused insanity. Those rays are also supposed to transform werewolves and vampires.

VOICES OF THE UNIVERSE

❝ It is the very error of the moon;
She comes more near the Earth than she was wont,
And makes men mad. **❞**

—**William Shakespeare,** *Othello*

Why is the Moon full of craters?

Craters are the result of asteroids or comets hitting the surface of a moon or planet. Space rocks come sailing into the Moon at top speeds because the Moon has no atmosphere to protect it. When a space rock slams into the Moon, it blasts a hole in the surface. The rock itself explodes, sending bits of rock and dust flying in every direction.

When does the Moon look like a big peach?

During a *lunar eclipse*, when Earth comes between the Sun and the Moon. With Earth blocking most of the Sun's light, the Moon glows a dark orange as just a little reddish light passes through our atmosphere to the Moon.

There are usually two partial or total lunar eclipses every year, and each lasts about four hours. Unlike solar eclipses, lunar eclipses are safe to look at with your eyes because moonlight is only a reflection of sunlight.

light outer shadow (*penumbra*)

dark inner shadow (*umbra*)

▲ A partial eclipse

Here is a list of total lunar eclipses in the next decade:

Date	Place
May 16, 2003	North and South America, Africa, Europe
November 9, 2003	North and South America, Africa, Europe, central Asia
May 4, 2004	South America, Africa, Europe, Asia, Australia
October 28, 2004	North and South America, Africa, Europe, central Asia
March 3, 2007	Africa, Europe, Asia, Australia
August 28, 2007	North and South America, east Asia, Australia
February 21, 2008	North and South America, Africa, Europe
December 21, 2010	North and South America, Europe, Asia, Australia

Who is the "man in the Moon"?

Many people think the face of a man smiles down from the surface of the Moon. The "face" comes from shadows cast by peaks and valleys on the surface of the Moon. Several peaks on the Moon approach the height of Mt. Everest, the tallest mountain on Earth. Those tall mountains were built when huge rocks smacked into the Moon billions of years ago. The Moon also has low-lying valleys and "seas." The seas aren't filled with water like ours on Earth (though astronomers once thought they might be). Instead, the seas are dark areas of smooth, hard lava that flowed into the basins after the impact of those huge rocks.

MARS

Size: 4,217 miles (6,786 km) across

Length of day: 24 hours, 37 minutes

Length of year: 687 Earth days

Distance from Sun: 142 million miles (228 million km)

Average surface temperature: -81 °F (-62 °C)

Number of known moons: 2

Number of known rings: 0

Weight of a 100-pound Earthling: 40 pounds (18 kg)

Why are aliens in stories usually "Martians" and not "Venusians" or "Mercurians"?

Probably because scientists think there's a better chance of finding life on Mars than on any other planet. Even though today's Mars is a dry, dusty world, it wasn't always that way. Scientists think water is necessary for life, and we know that liquid water flowed on Mars millions of years ago, and maybe much more recently. The water is still there, frozen at the planet's icy poles and under its surface. Scientists have also found hints of recent volcanic activity on Mars, which might mean that the interior of the planet is warm enough for living things to survive.

What's the difference between a canal and a channel?

It's enough to cause an uproar. In 1877, an Italian astronomer named Giovanni Schiaparelli said that he saw straight, regular lines on the surface of Mars. He called the lines *canali,* meaning "channels," passageways created naturally by flowing water. About twenty years later, an American astronomer named Percival Lowell (1855–1916) mistranslated "channels" to mean "canals." The big difference is that "canals" are artificial waterways that would have been created by intelligent beings. Lowell devoted his career to mapping what he thought were irrigation canals built by Martians to nourish their crops. Photographs taken of Mars in the 1970s revealed that indeed the planet had "channels," but no "canals."

VOICES OF THE UNIVERSE

❝ I looked again at the cylinder, and ungovernable terror gripped me. I stood petrified and staring. **❞**

❝ A big grayish rounded bulk, the size of a bear, perhaps, was rising slowly and painfully out of the cylinder. As it bulged up and caught the light it glistened like wet leather. **❞**

❝ Two large dark-colored eyes were regarding me steadfastly. The mass that framed them, the head of the thing, was rounded and had, one might say, a face. . . . **❞**

—**H. G. Wells,** *The War of the Worlds*

The idea of Martian canals inspired H. G. Wells's novel *The War of the Worlds,* in which bug-eyed Martians leave their desert planet and come to take over the greener Earth. The book was so convincing that many people believed there really was intelligent life on Mars. To make matters worse, when an updated version of the book was read on the radio in 1938, some people thought Martians really were invading and fled their houses!

Why is Mars red?

a It's very hot.

b It's embarrassed.

c It's rusty.

d It's the mascot of Cincinnati's baseball team.

The answer is *c. The Red Planet* gets its color from iron oxide—rust—in its soil. Mars is a dusty, rusty, gusty, orangish-red desert that's even drier than the Sahara. Violent storms blow the reddish dust all around, so the sky is pink. Mars even glows red in our night sky. Since the planet's color reminded the Greeks of blood, they named the planet Ares, after their god of war—who was known to the Romans as Mars.

Though red often means something is "red hot," that's not true in the case of Mars. Mars is actually cooler than Earth because it's farther away from the Sun. The average temperature on the planet is -81 °F (-63 °C).

Have humans ever landed on Mars?

No, but there are plans to send people there in the early part of this century. First we have to make sure the astronauts won't get stranded without enough fuel to get home. The journey to Mars takes ten months—and that's just one way. We're not even sure that humans can stay healthy in space for as long as it takes to get to Mars and back. (So far, the longest anyone has been in space is 439 days, or about a year and three months.) Stay tuned for more developments.

What have space probes learned about Mars?

In the past decade, we've lost several probes that were sent to land on Mars. One failed because engineers made a math error. Another is supposed to have landed in an unmapped crater, and the fate of a third remains a mystery. Some people think the failures are a result of trying to do too much too quickly and too cheaply.

In 1976, two space probes named *Viking I* and *Viking II* landed on Mars. Each had a robot arm to scoop up Martian soil and a minilaboratory for experiments. The *Viking* landers tested the soil for signs of life, but none was found.

Almost twenty years later, in 1997, the spacecraft *Pathfinder* landed on Mars and released a small remote-controlled rover named *Sojourner*. *Sojourner* moved around the planet taking pictures, checking the weather, and studying the planet's soil and rocks. No signs of life were found by *Sojourner*, either. Some scientists think that there is life on Mars, but that we just haven't yet looked in the right places or with the right tools.

Do we have any Mars rocks on Earth?

We think so. No spacecraft has brought back rock samples from Mars like the ones astronauts have brought back from the Moon. But some Mars rocks may have made their way to Earth on their own. How? Scientists have found about a dozen rocks on Earth that may be meteorites from Mars. These are pieces of the planet that were chipped off by a collision with a space rock long ago. The rocks match samples of Martian soil analyzed by the *Viking* landers. Some scientists think that one such meteorite, found in Antarctica, may even contain fossils of tiny organisms called bacteria—but, as often happens, other scientists disagree.

Will humans ever live on Mars?

Maybe. Some people support plans to *terraform* Mars, or turn it into another version of Earth. To do that we'd have to raise temperatures on the Red Planet by releasing gases to trap the planet's heat and hold it within the atmosphere. That would make the frozen water melt so that plants could be grown. The plants would release oxygen for people to breathe.

Would there be good vacation spots on Mars?

If humans did ever move to Mars, the planet would be a great place to open some incredible national parks. Mars is home to Olympus Mons, the largest volcano in the solar system. Olympus Mons is three times as tall as Mt. Everest. Like all other volcanoes on Mars, Olympus Mons is *extinct*, which means it doesn't erupt anymore. Mars also boasts the deepest canyon in the solar system, Valles Marineris. Marineris is four times as deep as the Grand Canyon and long enough to stretch clear across the United States.

CHAPTER 3

How's the Weather on Neptune?

JUPITER

Size: 86,885 miles (139,824 km) across

Length of day: about 10 Earth hours

Length of year: about 12 Earth years

Distance from Sun: 484 million miles (779 million km)

Average temperature at cloud tops: -243 °F (-153 °C)

Number of known moons: 17

Number of known rings: 2

Weight of a 100-pound Earthling: 249 pounds (113 kg)

Why is Jupiter called the "King of Planets"?

Because Jupiter is the largest planet in the solar system. It's so big that more than 1,300 Earths could fit inside it! Jupiter is also heavier than all the other planets combined. It makes sense that the "King of Planets" was named for the king of the Roman gods and goddesses.

Despite Jupiter's enormous size, it spins faster than any other planet. A day on Jupiter is about ten hours long.

▲ Earth

▲ Jupiter

How far could you walk on Jupiter?

Not very far, because there'd be nothing solid to walk *on*! Jupiter is made mostly of gas and hot, liquid hydrogen. But even if Jupiter did have a surface to stand on, you wouldn't last there very long before you'd be crushed by the planet's enormous gravity and pressure. At 12,000 miles (20,000 km) beneath the cloud tops, the air pressure is three million times that of Earth.

Why does Jupiter look different every night?

Because every night is a stormy night on Jupiter. When you look at Jupiter through a telescope, you see a planet covered with thick red, orange, brown, and white clouds. Fierce winds blow bands of multicolored clouds around the planet, so the planet looks a little different each night. The winds swing around Jupiter's Great Red Spot, a huge storm that's been raging nonstop for at least three hundred years. That storm alone is about two times the size of Earth. No one is sure if or when the Great Red Spot will ever disappear.

What would you see on a clear night on Jupiter?

Do you remember which scientist discovered these four large moons with his homemade telescope in 1609? Here's a hint: the moons are called the *Galilean moons*.

Galileo

A sky full of moons. Jupiter has seventeen moons, and the four largest are some of the most unusual bodies in the solar system:

Ganymede is the solar system's biggest moon. It's even bigger than the planets Pluto and Mercury. Ganymede has a thin atmosphere and dirty ice on its surface.

Europa is covered with a smooth layer of ice that might have an ocean under it, like Earth's Arctic Ocean.

Io is a cosmic polluter. It's the most volcanic world in the solar system. Instead of Earth-type lava, Io's volcanoes spew sulfurous lava (which smells like rotten eggs) onto its surface and into space.

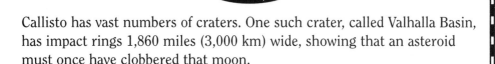

Callisto has vast numbers of craters. One such crater, called Valhalla Basin, has impact rings 1,860 miles (3,000 km) wide, showing that an asteroid must once have clobbered that moon.

SATURN

Size: 74,900 miles (120,536 km) across

Length of day: about 11 Earth hours

Length of year: about 29 Earth years

Distance from Sun: 889 million miles (1.43 billion km)

Average temperature at cloud tops: -300 °F (-184 °C)

Number of known moons: 22

Number of known rings: 7 major ones that contain thousands of ringlets

Weight of a 100-pound Earthling: 110 pounds (50 kg)

Is Saturn unsinkable?

Yes. Even though Saturn is almost as big as its neighbor, Jupiter, it is much less *dense*: the liquid and gas it is made of are packed together quite loosely. Saturn has such a low density, in fact, that if you could find an ocean big enough to put it in, the planet would float.

How many rings does Saturn have?

Only seven rings have been seen from Earth, but a space probe passing near Saturn showed that these are put together from thousands of separate ringlets. Though the rings look solid from far away, each one is actually made of billions of icy rocks. Some of those pieces are as small as a grain of sand, while others are as large as a house. Every single piece has its own orbit around Saturn, like a very tiny moon.

Saturn's rings are extremely thin. Though they stretch for more than 124,000 miles (200,000 km) into space, they are only 100 feet (30 m) thick. Trying to see them from the edge is like trying to spot the edge of a CD from 20 miles (32 km) away.

Why do some planets have rings, while others don't?

It's all about gravity. All the giant planets in our solar system—Jupiter, Saturn, Uranus, and Neptune—have rings. (Though Saturn's are by far the most spectacular.) That's because the giant planets all have strong gravitational pulls. Scientists think the rings' ice and rock particles may be chips knocked off the planets' moons. In the case of Saturn, they may be the remains of a smashed moon or comet.

▲ An artist's conception of the *Voyager 2* mission, which explored the gaseous planets

Who solved the mystery of Saturn's "ears"?

When Galileo saw Saturn through a telescope in 1610, he was confused by the planet's shape. He thought Saturn had "ears," or handles like a teacup, because it looked like the planet's rings were attached to it. The mystery was solved in 1655, when Dutch astronomer Christian Huygens built a better telescope that helped him discover the truth.

Do Saturn's rings have sheep?

No, but they do have shepherds. Two tiny moons called Prometheus and Pandora orbit Saturn on either side of one of its narrow rings. They are called "shepherding moons" because their combined gravity keeps this ring on a path that is only 60 miles (100 km) wide.

What's unique about Saturn's largest moon, Titan?

Titan, like Earth, has a dense atmosphere. Made mainly of nitrogen and methane gases, this atmosphere has some chemicals that can form the building blocks of life. In 2004, the spacecraft *Cassini* will reach Titan and release a probe named *Huygens*. The probe will parachute onto the mysterious moon and send back pictures and data.

Phoebe, Saturn's farthest moon, may be an asteroid captured by Saturn's gravity. For some reason, Phoebe orbits the opposite way from all of Saturn's other moons.

URANUS

Size: 31,770 miles (51,118 km) across

Length of day: about 17 Earth hours

Length of year: about 84 Earth years

Distance from Sun: 1.78 billion miles (2.87 billion km)

Average temperature at cloud tops: -353 °F (-214 °C)

Number of known moons: 21

Number of known rings: 11

Weight of a 100-pound Earthling: 90 pounds (41 kg)

What was new and different about the way Uranus was discovered?

Uranus was the first planet to be discovered with a telescope. When astronomer William Herschel first spotted Uranus in 1781, he thought he'd found a comet. When he realized he'd discovered a whole new planet, the solar system got twice as big. That's because Uranus is twice as far away from the Sun as its neighbor Saturn. Uranus is so far away, in fact, that through Earthbound telescopes the icy planet looks like a tiny disk.

Herschel wanted to name the new planet "George's Star," after King George III of England. (Can you imagine: Mercury, Venus, Earth, Mars, Jupiter, Saturn, and . . . George?) Herschel couldn't get enough astronomers to agree that the king of England should have his own planet, so Uranus was named after the Roman god who was the father of Saturn and grandfather of Jupiter.

William (1738–1822) and **Caroline** (1750–1848) **Herschel**

Sir Frederick William Herschel and his sister Caroline Lucretia Herschel were born in Germany but spent most of their lives in England, where they had moved to work as professional musicians. William became so fascinated by telescopes that he decided to build his own. Since they didn't have much money, he and Caroline used horse manure as a mold for the telescopes' mirrors. Their 4-foot-wide, 40-foot-long telescope was the largest in the world at the time. It let the astronomers see farther into space than anyone before them.

Even when William could afford to buy telescopes, he preferred to build them himself. He hand-ground his own lenses and mirrors, a delicate process that could take sixteen hours. While he was grinding, Caroline spoon-fed her brother to keep up his strength. Caroline was also an able astronomer who discovered eight comets herself. The royal pensions awarded to her and her brother by King George III after the discovery of Uranus made Caroline the first female professional astronomer.

VOICES OF THE UNIVERSE

❝ Seeing is in some respect an art, which must be learnt. To make a person see with such a power is nearly the same as if I were to make him play one of Handel's fugues upon the organ. **❞**

—**William Herschel**, writing about the power to see through his new telescope

How is Uranus like a carnival ride?

Compared to the other planets, Uranus is spinning on its side. From Earth, the planet's eleven rings seem to go around it up and down like a Ferris wheel, instead of side to side like a merry-go-round. No one knows why this is so. Some astronomers think a planet-sized object may have knocked Uranus onto its side long ago.

Where can you find monster clouds in a blue-green sky?

On Uranus, where towering clouds as big as the continent of Europe form in the chilly atmosphere. Like its giant neighbors in the solar system, Uranus has a small, rocky core surrounded by vast amounts of liquid and gas. Traces of methane gas in the planet's hydrogen atmosphere reflect blue light, giving the planet a lovely aqua color.

Does Uranus have an inside-out moon?

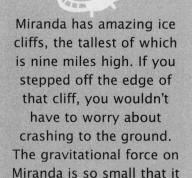

Miranda has amazing ice cliffs, the tallest of which is nine miles high. If you stepped off the edge of that cliff, you wouldn't have to worry about crashing to the ground. The gravitational force on Miranda is so small that it would take you about half an hour to float to the canyon floor below!

It sure does: Miranda. Uranus has twenty-one moons, but Miranda is the strangest of them all. It looks like a badly made jigsaw puzzle. Some of the moon's insides are on its outside, and some pieces of its surface are nowhere to be found. Scientists think Miranda was probably broken apart by a collision with another body and then brought back together by gravity.

NEPTUNE

Size: 30,776 miles (49,528 km) across

Length of day: about 16 Earth hours

Length of year: about 165 Earth years

Distance from Sun: 2.79 billion miles (4.5 billion km)

Average temperature at cloud tops: -373 °F (-225 °C)

Number of known moons: 8

Number of known rings: 4

Weight of a 100-pound Earthling: 110 pounds (50 kg)

▲ One *Voyager 2* view of Neptune

How was math the path to Neptune?

Neptune was the first planet discovered using mathematics. About 150 years ago, astronomers realized there was something mysterious about the planet Uranus. Its orbit around the Sun did not follow the path predicted by Newton's and Kepler's laws of gravitation. One explanation: the gravity from another big planet was pulling on Uranus and disturbing its orbit. So mathematicians figured where such a planet would be, and in 1846 German astronomer Johann Galle pointed his telescope there. Wow! There was Neptune, glowing like a faint blue-green star. The new aqua-colored planet was named after the Roman god of the sea.

Who discovered Neptune's rings?

It's not a "who," but a "what." A space probe named *Voyager 2* discovered Neptune's four rings in 1989. On its way to Neptune, *Voyager* toured Jupiter, Saturn, and Uranus. The probe took advantage of a rare line-up of the gas giants that created a sort of superhighway to speed the trip. The gravity of the giant planets helped push the probe on its way.

How's the weather on Neptune?

It's pretty awful! Neptune has the fiercest, fastest winds in the solar system. The supercold gales can whip around the planet at more than 1,250 miles per hour (2,000 km per hour). The Neptune forecast usually calls for storms, storms, and more storms. The storms come and go, but three we can sometimes see on Neptune's surface are the Earth-sized Great Dark Spot; the Moon-sized Small Dark Spot; and smaller Scooter, a speedy white storm that seems to chase the other storms around the planet!

Neptune's weather puzzles astronomers, because they don't know where the planet gets the energy to power the storms. Storms are usually caused by heat from the Sun. But Neptune is so far away that very little of the Sun's energy reaches it. Curious scientists may have to wait quite a while to have their questions answered, since the planet won't be in a convenient alignment for launching a probe for more than a hundred years.

Neptune's moon Triton is the coldest place in the solar system. Its temperatures can get as low as -391 °F (-235 °C). It's so cold there that Triton's volcanoes spew frozen nitrogen instead of molten lava. Still, for frigid Triton to show any activity at all is remarkable. Scientists think it must be heated inside.

How is Neptune like a jewelry store?

It's full of diamonds—or so some scientists think. In the intense pressure of Neptune's inner atmosphere, carbon atoms in the air might stick together, forming diamond crystals. Neptune's sky could literally rain diamonds. However, if you were in such a nasty, crushing, poisonous place, you probably wouldn't care.

PLUTO

Size: 1,480 miles (2,400 km) across

Length of day: about 6 Earth days

Length of year: about 248 Earth years

Average distance from Sun: 3.73 billion miles (6 billion km)

Average surface temperature: -243 °F (-153 °C)

Number of known moons: 1

Number of known rings: 0

Weight of a 100-pound Earthling: 7 pounds (3 kg)

 Pluto is the farthest planet from the Sun.

True . . . and false! Pluto is *usually* the farthest planet from the Sun. But sometimes Neptune is the farthest, because Pluto's odd orbit takes it inside Neptune's orbit for about 20 out of every 250 years. The last time this happened was from 1979 to 1999. Even though the two outermost planets travel in the same area, they'll never hit each other because they don't actually cross paths. Pluto's orbit, instead of being flat, is tilted like a ramp compared to the orbits of the other planets.

When Pluto is at the farthest reach of its orbit, it's fifty times farther from the Sun than Earth is.

 Astronomers aren't sure if Pluto is:

a. a planet

b. Mickey Mouse's favorite dog

c. the last planet in the solar system

d. smooth or cratered

e. all of the above

The answer is *e*. (Well, the jury's still out on the dog issue.) There's a lot we don't know about Pluto. That's because the planet was only discovered in 1930, and it's just so far away. Pluto was found because astronomers were investigating a gravitational force that seemed to be pulling on the existing planets. American astronomer Clyde Tombaugh, searching for a ninth planet that might be exerting this force, found Pluto the same way Johann Galle had found Neptune—from mathematical predictions of where it should be. Tombaugh began to look through photographs of the sky to see if he could find an object that was moving against the background of stars. He found it—a tiny, dim, starlike wanderer.

Yet, strangely, tiny Pluto turned out not to have nearly enough mass to cause the gravitational pull astronomers had found. Tombaugh had found a planet, but not the one he was looking for. (Later, it turned out that this extra gravitational pull didn't really exist. Astronomers had just made some mistakes in measuring the orbit of Uranus.)

Some astronomers aren't even convinced that Pluto is actually a planet. In fact, the American Museum of Natural History in New York City has gone so far as to remove Pluto from its planetary exhibits. Pluto is so small (less than two-thirds the size of our Moon) and has such a strange orbit that these astronomers think the icy little ball might be a body from the solar system's Kuiper Belt (see page 66), captured by the gravity of Neptune.

So what *do* we know about Pluto?

We know that it's very dark, very cold, very small, and very hard to see. Tiny Pluto is so far away that, even with a telescope, observing it is like trying to read the writing on a postage stamp from forty miles away! That's why a little girl in England suggested the planet be named for the Roman god who ruled the dark and mysterious underworld.

Astronomers believe that Pluto's surface is covered with ice and snow, including two polar ice caps. It even has an atmosphere, but not much of one. When Pluto is farthest from the Sun, its thin air must freeze and collapse into an icy drift on the planet's surface.

▲ An artist's rendering of the *Pluto-Kuiper Express* nearing Pluto and Charon

We should know more about Pluto one day because early in this century, a probe called *Pluto-Kuiper Express* will be launched to travel as quickly as possible to the farthest planet. At the time the *Express* is planned to arrive, around 2020, Pluto will still be fairly close to us.

Does Pluto have a twin?

Pluto and its moon Charon (KAR-uhn) are like a double planet because they are close in size (Charon is half as big as Pluto). The two bodies orbit so closely that they're locked facing each other: if you stood on Pluto, the moon would never rise or set, but would appear to hover motionless in the sky.

Asteroids, Meteoroids, and Comets

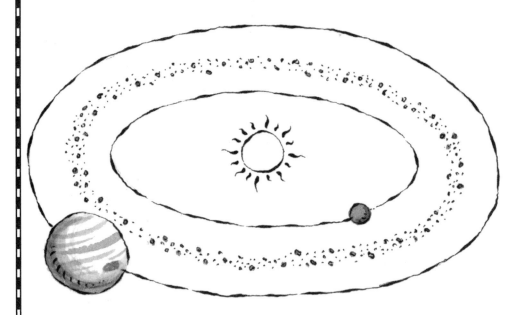

Where do asteroids like to hang out?

Asteroids, or "minor planets," can be found all over the solar system, but most orbit the Sun in an *asteroid belt* between Mars and Jupiter. Asteroids are space rocks that never formed into a planet when the solar system was born. This is probably because of the gravitational effects of Mars and Jupiter. Even if the asteroids *had* become a planet, they'd be less than one quarter the size of Earth.

How many asteroids are out there?

Astronomers have found more than 20,000 asteroids since 1801 and discover more every year. The largest asteroid, Ceres, was the first one found. Ceres is almost 600 miles (970 km) across, or about one quarter of the size of our Moon. But that's pretty unusual. Though a few asteroids are 150 miles (240 km) across or more, most are less than a few miles wide and many are smaller than a car. There are more small asteroids than large ones because the space rocks often crash into each other and break into smaller pieces. (The little pieces become meteoroids, some of which are sent on a path toward Earth.) That's also why most asteroids are lopsided and full of craters.

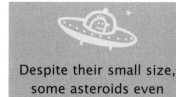

Despite their small size, some asteroids even have their own tiny moons!

Did an asteroid kill the dinosaurs?

Many scientists think so. The paths of some asteroids do cross Earth's orbit. If a huge asteroid hit the dinosaur-inhabited Earth 65 million years ago, it could have thrown so much dust into the air that the Sun's light was dimmed. In time, the Earth might have become so cold that the change in climate would have killed the dinosaurs.

I have a head and a tail, I can move around, but you can't take me for a walk. What am I?

▲ Tail   ▲ Head

A comet. Comets are dirty, rocky snowballs that orbit the Sun. They spend most of their lives far away from us, but when a comet's orbit brings it near the Sun, part of its frozen "head" defrosts into a dusty, gaseous "tail" millions of miles long. Then the comet appears as a brilliant streak we can see in the sky for weeks or even months. Since the pressure of the Sun's radiation—which is what pushes the dust and gas away from the comet—always flows away from the Sun, the comet's tail always points away from the Sun, too. That means that sometimes the comet seems to travel backward, with the tail leading the head!

Where do comets come from?

Most astronomers think that comets come from two places: the Oort Cloud, a huge icy ring around the edge of the solar system, and the Kuiper Belt, a ring of planetary leftovers inside the Oort Cloud. Comets that come in our direction have probably been pulled in slowly because of the gravitational tugs of planets or passing stars.

If you discover a comet, you get your name in lights—the comet is named after you (and whoever sees it at the same time). That's why some comets have names like Shoemaker-Levy or Hale-Bopp.

All comets orbit the Sun in a predictable *period,* or amount of time. Short-period comets orbit at least once every 200 years and probably come from the Kuiper Belt. Long-period comets take more than 200 years and most likely come from the Oort Cloud.

Edmond Halley (1656–1742)

As a student at Oxford University in England, Edmond Halley (rhymes with valley) was so excited about astronomy that he left school to map the stars in the Southern Hemisphere's skies. Halley is best known for his groundbreaking work on comets, especially the one that bears his name. Halley was the first to say that comets sighted in 1531, 1607, and 1682 were actually the same comet returning every 76 years. He predicted the comet's return in 1758, though he knew he wouldn't live to see the prediction come true. When it did, the comet was named in his honor.

Astronomy was just one of Edmond Halley's many strengths. Among countless other things, he developed the first weather map and studied Earth's magnetic field. The multitalented Halley was England's Astronomer Royal from 1719 until he died in 1742 at Greenwich Observatory in England.

Who's coming to visit in 2062?

Halley's Comet, the most famous of them all. Halley's visits have been connected to several historic events. The Chinese saw the comet in 240 B.C. and blamed it for the death of an empress. The Romans recorded it in 12 B.C. and thought it was connected to the death of one of their statesmen. In 1066, the Normans of France believed the comet marked the invasion of England by William the Conqueror. (The comet is even shown on the Bayeux Tapestry, which records William's victory.) Halley's Comet also came through the years the famous American writer Samuel Clemens—also known as Mark Twain—was born and died.

Could an asteroid strike the Earth?

It's very unlikely, but it could happen. In fact, some scientists think that a small asteroid or large meteoroid blew up in Earth's atmosphere and created a huge ring of destruction in the Tunguska region of Siberia in 1908. Eyewitnesses saw a huge fireball move across the sky, followed by a brilliant explosion that lasted only an instant. The blast, the largest ever recorded on Earth, sent shock waves around the world. It burned and blew down trees for twenty miles around. People and animals were knocked off their feet 37 miles (60 km) from the site.

No one is sure what caused the explosion, but many scientists think it was a small asteroid that exploded in the air, creating a bomblike airburst. There was no significant impact crater at the site: whatever the body was, it did not hit the ground.

VOICES OF THE UNIVERSE

❝I had just raised my axe . . . when suddenly . . . the sky was split in two, and high above the forest the whole northern part of the sky appeared to be covered with fire. At that moment I felt a great heat as if my shirt had caught fire. . . . I wanted to pull off my shirt and throw it away, but at that moment there was a bang in the sky, and a mighty crash was heard. I was thrown on the ground. . . . The crash was followed by a noise like stones falling from the sky, or guns firing. The Earth trembled. . . .❞

—A report from an eyewitness of the Tunguska event

In 1994, astronomers watched Comet Shoemaker-Levy smash into Jupiter. That was the only time scientists had ever witnessed a big celestial object collide with any body in the solar system. Shoemaker-Levy caused huge explosions in Jupiter's atmosphere. Black scars the size of Earth stayed visible for more than a year.

▲ Artist's rendering showing the collision of a comet with Jupiter

 You can catch a shooting star.

True. It's actually more likely that one would land on you as a speck of dust and you wouldn't even know it. But if you did catch one, you'd see that a shooting star isn't a star at all. It's a piece of space dust called a *meteoroid*. Meteoroids are chips and chunks knocked off asteroids and comets by collisions.

When a meteoroid enters Earth's atmosphere and tunnels through the air, it gets so hot that it becomes a brilliant streak of light in the sky—a shooting star, or *meteor*. Many meteors burn up in our atmosphere, but some land on Earth. These are called *meteorites*. Most meteorites are tiny, but some are as big as baseballs, bowling balls, or even buildings. Many natural history museums have meteorites on display.

Away from city lights on a clear night, you should be able to see about three to five meteors an hour. But at certain times of the year, when Earth passes through the dust and debris of a comet, you can see many more. The meteors in these *meteor showers* seem to radiate from one spot in the sky, like the water from a shower head. Meteor showers happen at the same time every year. Each takes its name from the constellation it appears to come from. Check out this list, and make a wish!

Shower	Approx. Date	Approx. Number per Hour	Parent Comet
Quadrantids	January 3	40	
Lyrids	April 22	15	Comet Thatcher
Eta Aquarids	May 4	20	Comet Halley
Delta Aquarids	July 30	20	
Perseids	August 12	50	Comet Swift-Tuttle
Orionids	October 21	25	Comet Halley
Taurids	November 4	15	Comet Encke
Leonids	November 16	15	Comet Temple-Tuttle
Geminids	December 13	50	3200 Phaethon
Ursids	December 22	20	Comet Tuttle

Has anyone ever been hit by a meteorite?

Yes. About a dozen people have been hit by meteorites in the past 500 years, including at least one person in the United States. (An Alabama woman received a badly bruised thigh when a meteorite came crashing through her ceiling in 1954.) No human is known to have been killed by a meteorite, but a dog was killed in Egypt in 1911.

That record's not too bad when you consider that thousands of meteorites have been found worldwide. Antarctica is one of the best places to look for meteorites because they stand out against the white ice. The largest known meteorite on Earth was found in Namibia, Africa, in 1920. That space boulder fell to Earth during prehistoric times and has never been moved. It's about 9 feet long and 8 feet wide (2.7 m long and 2.4 m wide), roughly the size of a small car, but weighs about 119,000 pounds (54,000 kg).

CHAPTER 4

HOW BIG IS THE UNIVERSE?

VOICES OF THE UNIVERSE

" We had the sky, up there, all speckled with stars, and we used to lay on our backs and look up at them, and discuss about whether they was made, or only just happened—Jim he allowed they was made, but I allowed they happened. . . . **"**

— **Mark Twain**, *Huckleberry Finn*

Stars

Why do stars shine?

They can't help it. Stars are so hot that they radiate huge amounts of *energy* in the form of light and heat.

A star is "born" inside a giant cloud of dust and gases. Gravity pulls the dust and gas together into a cool, loosely packed *protostar*, which is like a star-in-training. Over millions of years, the protostar pulls in more and more gas and contracts, getting smaller, denser, and hotter. It will begin to glow as it contracts. Finally gravity pressing on the core of the ball of gas heats it so much that *fusion* begins, making the star more stable. Atoms of hydrogen gas in the star's superhot core fuse, or stick together, to make helium atoms. In the process, they release energy. In our Sun, 600 million metric tons of hydrogen fuse into helium each second, making the enormous amount of heat and light that powers life on Earth.

What's the difference between stars and planets?

The main difference between the two is that stars make their own light and planets don't. Planets are too small to begin fusion in their cores. The smallest size a star could be and still shine is about 8 percent of our Sun's mass (or, about eighty times *more* massive than Jupiter, the largest of our planets). On the other hand, if a star gets too big, it would probably be blown apart by the force of its own energy. The largest known stars are one hundred times as massive as the Sun.

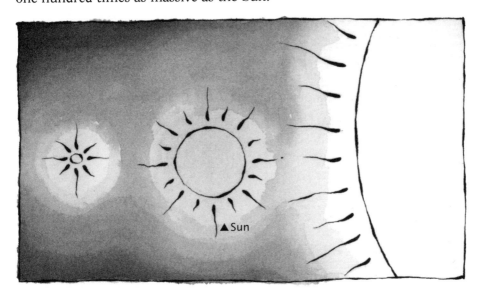

▲ Sun

Are stars really star-shaped?

Stars aren't alive, but they do have a lot in common with things that are. Stars are born, grow old, and die, just like people do. They come in all different colors. They live in neighborhoods. Many have lifelong mates. Some flare up from time to time. Some are predictable, others surprising. Some even appear to have a pulse.

No, they're actually round. The gravity of a star, like that of most bodies in space, pulls all its matter toward the center pretty evenly. (If this wasn't the case, we'd have planets and stars shaped like bananas, refrigerators, or stop signs!) Stars look star-shaped from Earth because the movement of air around our planet makes stars' steady light look like it's flickering, or twinkling. To astronauts, stars are steady dots of light.

How many stars can you see on a clear night, without a telescope?

That depends on where you are and how good your eyes are. If you're in a typical suburban neighborhood, you might only see about 200 stars. But if you're out in the country, where the glare of city lights doesn't get in the way, you'll see closer to 3,000. With binoculars, you can see five to ten times more stars, and with an amateur telescope, you can see about fifty times more. Still, that's only a fraction of the countless trillions of stars that exist in the universe. There are more stars in space than there are grains of sand on all the beaches on our entire planet.

Where are the stars during the day?

They're in the sky. You just can't see them. That's because the Sun's light blocks out the light from other stars.

How long is a light-year?

A light-year isn't a measure of time: it's a measure of distance. When things begin to be trillions of miles away, measuring in miles or kilometers is as silly as trying to measure the distance from New York to London in inches. That's where light-years come in. A *light-year* is the distance light travels in a year. That's almost 6 trillion miles (9.5 trillion kilometers), or an incredible 186,000 miles (299,000 km) a *second*. Light travels faster than anything else we know of in the universe.

The distance to the nearest star, Proxima Centauri, is about 25 trillion miles (40 million km). It seems much more manageable to say that it is 4.3 light-years away. In comparison, the Sun is a mere eight light-minutes from us.

Light travels so fast that it can go all the way around Earth seven and a half times in just one second. If you tried to drive a car around Earth going the speed your parents do on the highway, it would take about a month without any stops. At that same speed, it would take you 177 years to reach the Sun.

How is the sky like a time machine?

Looking at the stars is like looking back in time. That's because many of the stars are so far away that the starlight you see now started coming toward you hundreds, thousands, or even millions of years ago. The light from the stars in the Big Dipper left those stars between 78 and 124 years ago, probably during the time your great-great grandparents lived. The light you see now from the star Deneb, in the constellation Cygnus the Swan, started 1,600 years ago, in the last days of the Roman Empire. The light from the farthest thing you can see with your bare eyes, our neighbor the Andromeda galaxy (see page 91), left on its journey a whopping 2.3 million years ago, when woolly mammoths roamed Earth with our earliest ancestors.

 ## The brighter the star, the closer it is to Earth.

True and false. A star's brightness, as seen from Earth, depends both on how close the star is and how big and hot it is.

The first person to classify stars according to their brightness was the Greek astronomer Hipparchus. He rated the brightest stars magnitude 1, while the faintest stars that could be seen with the naked eye were magnitude 6. We still use Hipparchus's scale today for stars and planets, though it's been expanded in both directions. With binoculars you can see objects of about magnitude 9, and with an amateur telescope, even dimmer ones of magnitude 11 or more. The amazing Hubble Space Telescope, which orbits at the edge of Earth's atmosphere, can detect stars of a magnitude 29! At the other end of the spectrum, brightly shining Venus is about magnitude -4, the full Moon is about -12, and the Sun is a whopping -26.7.

Just to make things even more confusing, we can also measure a star by its *luminosity*, or how much energy it gives out compared to the Sun. You can think of luminosity like the wattage of a lightbulb. The Sun's luminosity is equal to about 4,000,000,000,000,000, 000,000,000 100-watt lightbulbs.

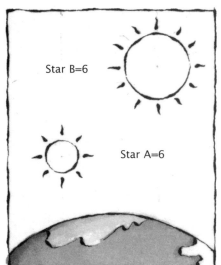

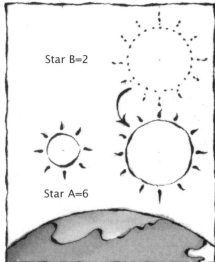

▲Apparent magnitude ▲Absolute magnitude

These numbers describe a planet or star's *apparent magnitude*, or how bright it *appears* to be from Earth. *Absolute magnitude* tells us how bright the object actually is, or how bright each star would be if every star were the same distance from us. See the illustration above: from Earth, star A and star B look equally bright—they have the same *apparent magnitude*. If star B were brought to the same distance as star A, we would see that it is much brighter and bigger, with a different *absolute magnitude*. The Sun's absolute magnitude is 4.83, so it's not all that bright compared to other stars. The star Deneb, for instance, has an absolute magnitude of –8.73.

Do stars come in rainbow colors?

They sure do. Though it might seem like all the stars are silver-white, if you look closely you'll see that some stars are red or orange, others are yellowish like the Sun, and still others are blue. That's because the stars are different temperatures. Their color tells you how hot they are and how much energy they're giving off. Blue stars are the hottest, followed by white, yellow, orange, and finally red. If you look closely (but not too closely!) at a campfire, you can see the same variation of colors in the flames.

The Sun gives off:

a radio waves   **c** light rays

b X rays   **d** all of the above

The answer is *d*. All these things are part of a wide range of *radiation*, or energy traveling in waves. Stars and other warm objects in space all give off radiation. Each kind of energy has its own set of wavelengths, the distance from the crest of one wave to the next.

At the high-powered end of the spectrum, with the shortest wavelengths, are gamma rays, then X rays. Both gamma rays and X rays can damage your cells, which is why you wear that heavy piece of fabric over your body when you get X rays at the dentist. We're protected from the Sun's X rays by Earth's atmosphere. Next come ultraviolet, or UV, rays, from which we're only partially protected. UV rays are the reason you wear sunscreen. Then comes the rainbow spectrum of visible light. Visible light is followed by infrared waves, which feel warm on your skin. Then come microwaves, and lastly radio waves, with the longest wavelengths and the least power. All these forms of radiation travel at the same speed—the speed of light.

COSMIC SUPERSTARS:

Henrietta Swan Leavitt (1868–1921)

Special kinds of stars called *Cepheid variables* are important rulers we can use to measure the distance to the stars. Cepheids are special stars because they grow brighter and dimmer at very regular intervals. Some take only a day to go from their brightest to dimmest, while others take more than fifty days.

The usefulness of Cepheids was discovered in 1908 by Harvard astronomer Henrietta Swan Leavitt. Although Leavitt was deaf, this did not stop her from attending Radcliffe College and becoming an astronomer in a time when few women were scientists. Leavitt discovered about 2,400 variable stars during her career. But her major contribution to astronomy came when she realized that there was a connection between the brightness of a Cepheid and how fast it varied from bright to dim and back again. Using this connection, she could compare the star's true brightness (absolute magnitude) to its apparent magnitude to find out its distance from Earth.

Knowing the distance to faraway stars paved the way for the discovery of galaxies beyond our own. Cepheids are telling us just how big the universe is.

Do stars get married?

They don't have wedding ceremonies, but some stars are so attracted to each other (by gravity, not love) that they spend their lives together. Most stars look like they're all alone in the sky, but in reality about half are part of star systems—pairs or groups of stars held together by gravity. Most systems are *binary*, or double, systems, but many are triples and some have four or more stars. The stars in each system whirl around each other like cosmic dance partners.

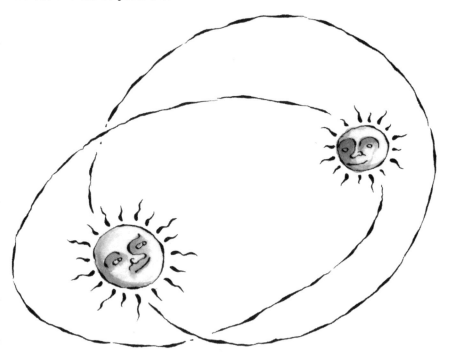

So where's the Sun's companion?

It doesn't have one. Not that we should complain—if it did, Earth might not have formed where it is! Our fairly ordinary star is slightly unusual in that way.

You can see a multiple star system on most clear nights. If you look closely at the middle star in the Big Dipper's handle, you'll see that it's really two stars lying close together instead of just one. The ancient Arabs and some Native American tribes considered the ability to make out these separate stars a good test of eyesight!

Are all binary stars what they appear to be?

No. Some play tricks on your eyes. Because of the position and angle of some binary star systems, one star will pass in front of the other as it orbits, dimming the companion star's light. These *eclipsing binaries* sometimes look like one star that's growing brighter and dimmer instead of two different stars.

On the other hand, some stars that look like binary systems really aren't. This happens when stars look close together in the sky, but one is actually much farther away than the other. These *optical doubles* might look like they're an orbiting pair, but they really aren't related at all.

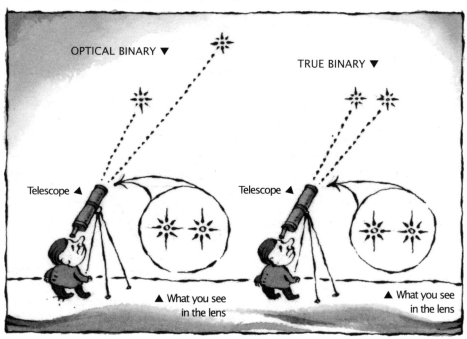

OPTICAL BINARY ▼

TRUE BINARY ▼

Telescope ▲

Telescope ▲

▲ What you see in the lens

▲ What you see in the lens

What would our constellations look like from somewhere else in the galaxy?

They definitely wouldn't look like they do from Earth.

Constellations are pictures people have imagined in the stars in much the same way you can imagine pictures in the clouds. Like optical doubles, the stars in any particular constellation only appear to be close together because they're in the same line of sight. In reality, some are much farther away than others.

Even our current views of the constellations as seen from Earth won't last forever. That's because, little by little, Earth changes its position among the stars in the Milky Way as our solar system moves around the galaxy. The change in our view can't be seen from year to year, but over time it adds up. In 100,000 years, for example, the Big Dipper's handle will be more bent and its bowl more pointed.

Constellations are useful for:

a playing connect-the-dots without wasting paper

b remembering characters for your Greek mythology test

c mapping the sky

The answer is *c*. Though constellations do make good connect-the-dots pictures, the images really make it easier to find and remember the positions of the stars in the sky.

People around the world have been imagining different star-pictures since ancient times. The constellations we know today come mainly from the Greeks. In A.D. 150, the great Greek astronomer and mathematician Ptolemy made a list of forty-eight constellations. Most of these are named after characters in Greek mythology. Some of the constellations look like the characters they're named for, but many don't.

Over time other skywatchers added more star-pictures. Today there are eighty-eight official constellations. In fact, modern astronomers have mapped the whole night sky into eighty-eight interlocking areas, each one named for the constellation it contains. Every single star in the sky, no matter how faint, is part of one constellation or another.

Polaris ▶

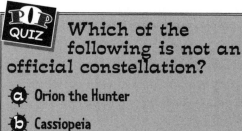

Which of the following is not an official constellation?

- **ⓐ** Orion the Hunter
- **ⓑ** Cassiopeia
- **ⓒ** Leo the Lion
- **ⓓ** the Big Dipper

Believe it or not, the answer is *d*. Some of the star-pictures that people think are constellations are really just a section of a constellation. The Big Dipper is part of the constellation Ursa Major, or Great Bear. The Little Dipper is part of Ursa Minor, the Little Bear. Star pictures that aren't officially constellations are called *asterisms*.

The bright North Star, also called Polaris because it's almost directly above Earth's North Pole, has helped travelers find their way for centuries. If you face the North Star, you're facing north. To find Polaris, trace a line with your finger from the front rim of the Big Dipper.

When can you see the constellations on parade?

All night, every night (when it's not cloudy). If you look at the stars at different times during the night, you'll see that the stars march across the sky. Because Earth is always rotating, the stars seem to rise, travel across the sky, and set just like the Sun. Because Earth is also in a slightly different position each night as the planet revolves around the Sun, the stars rise and set four minutes earlier than they did the night before. Over a year, that adds up to twenty-four hours and then the show begins again. So if you look at the stars every night at the same time for a year, you'll never see the same sky twice!

Who gets to name the stars?

The official star names used and recognized by scientists were either adopted long, long ago or have been published by observatories that specialize in star positions. Many of the names established by usage, like Betelgeuse, are Arabic. They come from the elaborate star charts the Arabs made about a thousand years ago. Other names come from a system introduced in the 1600s that combines Greek letters with the name of that star's constellation. (The Greek letters are often in order of brightness. Because alpha is the first letter in the Greek alphabet, Alpha Tauri is the brightest star in the constellation Taurus. Beta Tauri is the second brightest star in the constellation, and so on.) Still others have just been given numbers—as telescopes got bigger and better we could see more and more and more stars, and that seemed the simplest thing to do.

Can anyone name a star?

Sure, but the name won't be official. To raise money, some museums and astronomy and star stores will offer to "sell" you a star and let you name it. You'll just get a certificate to hang on your wall, but the name you picked won't be official. Only star names assigned by the International Astronomical Union (IAU), the worldwide federation of astronomical societies, are officially recognized by scientists. If you have your heart set on naming a heavenly body, you'll have to discover a comet.

TRUE OR FALSE

Massive stars live longer than less-massive stars.

False. Massive stars use up more fuel than less-massive ones, so they actually die sooner. The length of a star's life and what happens when it dies depend on how much mass the star has when it's born. Small stars are like small crowds of people—they tend to be much quieter than their larger counterparts. When a small or average-sized star, like the Sun, runs out of energy after billions of years, its outer layers expand and cool off. The star swells into a bright red ball called a *red giant*. As the red giant cools, its outer layers escape into space and the star becomes a small, gradually cooling *white dwarf*.

But when big stars die, you're in for some stellar fireworks—big stars go out with a bang. If a star is at least ten times more massive than the Sun, it may first swell into a red *supergiant* and then explode in a huge, brilliant explosion called a *supernova*. In an instant, a supernova releases a hundred times more energy than the Sun has radiated in its entire life. With the display over, a supernova collapses into either a small, hot, furiously spinning neutron star—or in the case of what was once a *really* big star, into a black hole.

White dwarfs are very small compared to normal stars. The brilliant star Sirius, for example, has a white dwarf companion no bigger than Earth. White dwarfs are also so dense—they have so much matter packed into a small space—that just a teaspoonful of one would weigh 2,000 pounds (900 kg) on Earth. That's as much as a small car. But that's nothing compared to the same amount of a neutron star, which would weigh 100 million times that much!

Do stars have babies?

No, though the ancients thought they did because some create *novas*, or bright flashes that can look like new stars. (*Nova* is Latin for "new.") Novas are different from supernovas. Novas happen in close binary star systems where one star is a small, dense white dwarf. Over time, the smaller star steals hot gas from the larger star. After a while, that extra mass creates so much pressure on the smaller star that the gassy layer blows up like a huge bomb. The star becomes thousands of times brighter than it was before. Then, if the bigger star still has enough mass left, the whole process may happen all over again, eventually creating another nova.

What do supernovas have to do with life on Earth?

Everything. Even though stars are mainly made of hydrogen and helium, when a supernova explodes it creates all the different elements found in the universe and blasts them out into space. Those elements form the building blocks of all the other objects in space—including Earth and the Moon, and even you and me. So you're literally made of stardust!

How is a neutron star like a lighthouse beacon?

Neutron stars spin incredibly fast—about a dozen times a second! As they do, the tiny stars—only 10 to 20 miles (16 to 32 km) wide—shoot out two narrow beams of radiation, such as light or radio waves. Depending on which way a neutron star is pointed, it can look like the star is flashing as the beams sweep past us on Earth. Like a lighthouse beacon, the light is "on" all the time, but we can only detect the radiation as it comes into our view. Neutron stars that appear to pulse with this regular energy are *pulsars*.

COSMIC SUPERSTARS:

Jocelyn Bell (1934–)

While she was a graduate student in astronomy at Cambridge University in England, Jocelyn Bell studied radio waves from space. To her surprise, she discovered in 1967 that some of these radio signals seemed to pulse out at very fast, regular intervals. Nothing in the universe was known to perform with the accuracy of these mysterious bodies. Astronomers only half-jokingly started calling them LGM1, LGM2, and so on, for "Little Green Men." While people knew that the pulses didn't really come from aliens, the LGMs remained a mystery until Bell and other astronomers realized they must be radiation from spinning neutron stars.

Are black holes black?

No, and they're not holes, either. A *black hole* is a collapsed, supermassive star whose gravity is so great that its matter is smooshed into an infinitely dense point smaller than the period at the end of this sentence. A black hole's gravity draws in everything that comes close enough and traps it forever. (One astronomer describes them as objects that dug a hole, jumped in, and then pulled the hole in after themselves!) To get out of a black hole, an object would have to travel faster than the speed of light. But since, as far as we know, that's impossible, not even light can escape a black hole, so the holes are invisible.

If black holes are invisible, how do we know they're there?

Looking for a black hole is like trying to find a black cat in a lightless cellar; we can't see it directly. One way astronomers try to detect black holes is by looking for the X rays they create. Gas pulled into a black hole would swirl around the hole like water around a bathtub drain. As it did, it would give off X rays. So astronomers look for strange X-ray sources in space as a signpost for black holes.

Another way astronomers have recently detected black holes is by looking out for what isn't there. To do this, they've compared two kinds of star systems: a sunlike star orbiting a neutron star and a sunlike star orbiting what they think is a black hole. The astronomers found that "nothing" definitely seemed to be something. The systems assumed to have a black hole gave off only 1 percent as much energy as those with a neutron star. Astronomers think that's because when the neutron star stole mass from the sunlike star, the matter of the two stars collided and gave off energy. When the black hole stole mass from the sunlike star, it gobbled the matter right up.

How close can you get to a black hole without being destroyed?

That depends on the size of the hole. Every black hole has an *event horizon*, an outer edge that's the last place light, gas, and matter can be detected. The event horizon of a black hole is the Point of No Return: once something crosses it, there's no turning back.

The width of a hole's event horizon depends on its mass. If a star ten times the size of the Sun collapsed into a black hole, its event horizon would be 37 miles (60 km) wide. If a million stars the size of the Sun collapsed into a black hole (which can happen at the center of a galaxy), then the black hole would be 3.7 billion miles (6 billion km) wide. Even a monster black hole like that one wouldn't drag in everything in the galaxy. Gravity from a black hole decreases with distance, just as it does for any body in the universe. You could safely look at a black hole—if you were far enough away.

Stephen Hawking (1942–)

British scientist Stephen Hawking was born three hundred years after Isaac Newton, and he also happens to hold the same position at Cambridge University that Newton once did. But unlike Newton, who'd never heard of a black hole (the theory of black holes was worked out in the early twentieth century), Hawking is the world's expert on these mass-eating mysteries.

Hawking knew by the time he was fourteen that he wanted to study math and physics. The focus of his life's work has been black holes, but he has also written several best-selling books about astronomy in general. While in graduate school at Cambridge, Hawking was diagnosed with Lou Gehrig's disease, an illness that disables the muscles but not the mind. Hawking was given two and a half years to live—and that was more than thirty years ago. Today Hawking is in a wheelchair and can't move very much or speak. He uses two fingers to tap out his thoughts on a computer keyboard and his words are then spoken by a computer voice.

Galaxies

How are stars like grapes?

They come in bunches. The universe is organized into millions of *galaxies*, large groups of stars held together by gravity. Most galaxies are grouped in *clusters*, and most clusters are grouped in *superclusters*. Scientists estimate that there are trillions or more galaxies in the visible universe, each with anywhere from billions to trillions of stars. Some galaxies are nicknamed for what they resemble—like Whirlpool, Black Eye, and Sombrero. Others are given letters and numbers, such as NGC 5128. Our galaxy is known as the Milky Way.

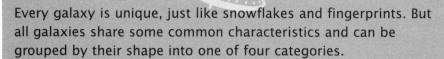

Every galaxy is unique, just like snowflakes and fingerprints. But all galaxies share some common characteristics and can be grouped by their shape into one of four categories.

Spiral galaxies

These galaxies are like giant, flat pinwheels with many arms that spin around a central core. They're home to stars of many ages. The Milky Way is one.

Barred spiral galaxies

These galaxies have a large bar running down the middle. Their arms trail from the bar like water from a lawn sprinkler.

Elliptical galaxies

These galaxies are home only to old stars. Some of them are egg shaped, others are nearly circular, and others are almost flat disks.

Irregular galaxies

These galaxies seem to have no shape at all. Some astronomers think they may not have enough stars to develop a specific form.

▲ A magnificent view of a spiral galaxy, 60 million light-years away

Do we live at the center of the Milky Way?

Until about a hundred years ago, astronomers thought we did. Just like we once put Earth at the center of the solar system, we also put our solar system at the center of the Milky Way. But our Sun is really way off to the side of the galaxy. We're on the Milky Way's Orion arm, about 28,000 light-years from the center. In this position, we slowly revolve around the Milky Way's center. The Milky Way turns only once every 230 million years, so the last time we were in the place we are now was when dinosaurs roamed Earth.

How big is the Milky Way?

The Milky Way is about 100,000 light-years across and 6,000 light-years deep at its thick middle section. (Like other spiral galaxies, the Milky Way has a bulge at its center. Many astronomers say that, from the outside, the Milky Way would look like two fried eggs stuck together.)

The Milky Way might seem huge—and it is to us. But at the same time, if the universe were the size of a football stadium, the Milky Way wouldn't even be as big as a pinhead.

Why is our galaxy called the Milky Way?

Not because it looks like a candy bar. The Milky Way gets its name from the milky band of light we see across the sky on a clear, dark night. That band is the central plane of our galaxy, the flattened disk that holds almost all of the galaxy's stars. In ancient times, people thought the glowing band looked like a river of milk. Greek legend said the Milky Way was the path to the palace of the god Zeus. The Romans thought it was a trail of wheat scattered by the harvest goddess. Other cultures thought it was a seam in the heavenly tent, or a path traveled by the dead. No one knew that the river of light was really a huge mass of stars until Galileo pointed his telescope at the sky in 1609.

Even though we know what the Milky Way is, we still don't know for sure what lies at its center. It probably contains clouds of dust and gas and a collection of star clusters. Gas circling at high speeds in the center of the galaxy suggests that there's a huge black hole there with the mass of 2.6 million Suns.

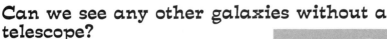

Can we see any other galaxies without a telescope?

Yes. Using our eyes alone, we can see our four closest neighbors in the Local Group. If you live in the *Southern Hemisphere*, or southern half, of Earth, you can see the Large and Small Magellanic Clouds, two dwarf irregular galaxies that orbit our galaxy. If you live in the *Northern Hemisphere*, you can see the Andromeda galaxy and, very faintly, the Triangulum galaxy. At more than 2 million light-years away, Andromeda is the closest major galaxy to ours. Astronomers call Andromeda our sister galaxy because they

Edwin Hubble saw that other galaxies were moving away from us by observing the galaxies' *redshift*. Redshift is an increase in the wavelength of radiation that happens when an object in space is moving away from the observer.

think the large spiral is almost a twin of the Milky Way. Since we can't see the Milky Way from the outside, we try to learn about it by observing Andromeda and others instead.

COSMIC SUPERSTARS:

Edwin Hubble (1889–1953)

American astronomer Edwin Hubble wanted to be a football player, but his mother disapproved. Hubble went to Oxford University in England to study law, and then returned to the United States to study the stars as well. It's a good thing for science that Hubble listened to his mother, since he went on to make some of the most important discoveries of the twentieth century.

While working at California's Mount Wilson Observatory in 1923, Hubble changed our view of the universe forever. For a long time, astronomers had thought the Milky Way was the whole universe instead of just a tiny part of it. They didn't know that other galaxies existed. Hubble used Mount Wilson's eight-foot-wide telescope, the world's largest at the time, to discover that the group of stars called Andromeda was really a galaxy, like our own.

Not only did Hubble then discover many other faraway galaxies, he found that all those galaxies were moving away from us at a speed that was related to their distance. Far-off galaxies were moving much more rapidly than closer galaxies. Hubble's discoveries gave us a key to the age and size of the universe and led to the development of the Big Bang theory of how the universe began. (See page 94.)

The far-sighted Hubble Space Telescope, which has revealed countless new wonders about the universe, is appropriately named in his honor. (You'll find more about the Hubble Telescope on page 103.)

If all the other galaxies are moving away from us, are we at the center of the universe?

No, though it does seem like this would be true. Since the universe is expanding, everything in it is moving away from everything else. A simple experiment will show this a bit more clearly: Take a deflated balloon and a permanent marker. Draw galaxies on the balloon, then blow the balloon up. As the balloon gets bigger, all your galaxies move farther and farther apart. This is the same thing that's happening in the universe.

How do today's astronomers see galaxies as they were billions of years ago?

Looking at faraway galaxies is just like looking at faraway stars. If a galaxy is a million light-years away, light that left that galaxy a million years ago is just now reaching us. So we see the galaxy as it was a million years ago. By studying galaxies that are at different distances from Earth (and thus appear at different ages), astronomers are now learning how galaxies change over time. By studying the farthest galaxies we can see, scientists may learn about the early days of the universe.

Why are some very distant galaxies so bright?

The farthest galaxies are about ten billion light-years away. If we can see them from so far away, these galaxies must be very, very bright. These galaxies are *active galaxies*, which send out massive amounts of radiation (light, radio waves, or X rays) from their centers. The centers of these active galaxies are called *quasars*, a term made up from "quasi-stellar radio source." Quasars are probably the result of huge amounts of matter disappearing into massive black holes. As the black hole sucks in the matter around it, some matter bounces back before it reaches the hole. This creates jets of energy equal to that of 1,000 galaxies put together.

The Universe and Its Mysteries

 ## Which of the following are part of the universe?

a planets, stars, mountains, and trees

b people, puppies, bikes, and computers

c heat, light, X rays, dust, and gas between the stars

d sounds, songs, movies, and dreams

e all of the above

The answer is *e*. The universe is everything that exists.

What is cosmology?

Cosmology is the branch of astronomy that asks the Big Questions. Its goal is to find the origins and structure of the universe. How did it begin, and how will it end? How big is it? How do its pieces work together? How do we fit into it all? These age-old cosmic mysteries are studied by cosmologists, a group of scientists that includes not only astronomers but also physicists and mathematicians.

Outer space might seem empty, but it is full of heat, light, X rays, gas clouds, tiny particles, and space debris.

How old is the universe?

Most scientists think the universe was born in a huge burst of energy about 13 billion years ago. Even though that burst is called the *Big Bang*, the "bang" wasn't an explosion that sent matter flying apart. Instead, it was a sudden expansion of space that carried matter and energy with it. After millions of years, pieces of the scattered matter clumped together, and stars began to shine.

Where did the universe come from?

The expansion of space that was the Big Bang started from a hot, heavy speck much smaller than an atom, into which all matter and energy were tightly packed. Nobody knows exactly what the speck was or why it began to expand. We also don't know what, if anything, existed before the Big Bang, because there was no time or space in our universe before it.

Some astronomers say the universe is 13 billion years old and 13 billion light-years wide. Others might say 12 billion, 15 billion, or 18 billion. We won't really know how old and big the universe is until we know for sure how fast the universe is expanding. So the dates you see for the age of the universe and the distances to very remote galaxies are just good estimates, for now.

VOICES OF THE UNIVERSE

❝ The eternal mystery of the world is its comprehensibility. . . . The fact that it is comprehensible is a miracle. ❞

—**Albert Einstein,** *Journal of the Franklin Institute*

Have we made a map of the universe?

We've started, but we've got a long way to go. Several groups of astronomers began mapping pie-shaped wedges of the universe in the 1980s. So far, even though they've mapped tens of thousands of galaxies, they've only covered a piece that's like the area of Vermont compared to the entire area of Earth!

Will the universe be around forever?

No one knows. Most scientists agree that what happens to the universe depends on how much matter it holds, and that's something we're not sure of yet. But there are probably three choices:

If there is precisely the right amount of matter—an unknown quantity scientists call *omega*—the universe will gradually slow down, stopping at an unimaginable, infinite time in the future.

If there is less matter than the omega amount, the universe will keep expanding forever. Matter will cool as it moves farther and farther apart and eventually stars will die out. This is called the *open universe model*.

If there is more than the omega amount of matter, gravity will one day stop the universe from expanding and draw the matter back together in a "Big Crunch." This is called the *closed universe model*.

Some scientists think that a Big Crunch might be more of a "Big Bounce," with all the matter in the universe coming together only to create another Big Bang—and another universe.

What is dark matter?

No one knows what it is, but theoretically it makes up at least 90 percent of the universe. For many years, astronomers have been puzzled by the way galaxies move and spin. The galaxies behave as though they have a lot more mass than the stars and gas clouds we can see. In fact, when we add up the detectable mass of all the visible objects in the universe, we can only account for about 6 or 7 percent of the mass that must exist in the universe. So most astronomers think that the universe is filled with *dark matter*: mass that we can't detect—so far.

What are MACHOs and WIMPs?

Astronomers have all kinds of ideas about what dark matter might be. The most likely candidates fall into two categories: MACHOs and WIMPs.

MACHOs are Massive Compact Halo Objects, or objects with substantial mass. These might be large planets, brown or black dwarfs, or black holes with nothing nearby to "eat" and therefore no radiation.

WIMPs are Weakly Interacting Massive Particles, or strange, tiny particles much smaller than atoms. Uncountable numbers of these WIMPs might make up the missing matter.

Dark matter might also include huge numbers of *neutrinos*. Neutrinos are particles left over from the Big Bang or spit out by the nuclear fusion going on inside stars. Neutrinos zip around at or near the speed of light, passing right through matter as if it weren't even there. They pass through Earth, and they pass through you. Scientists think that about 500 billion neutrinos made by the Sun pass through every inch of your body every second!

Is time travel possible?

A few people think so. They suggest that black holes are gates to other universes or shortcuts through time and space. These theories say that the infinitely dense center of a black hole might actually punch through to another place in time or space. These space-time tunnels are called *wormholes*. Matter that falls through a black hole would have an Alice-in-Wonderland-like experience, coming out in another universe in a "white hole." The famous scientist Albert Einstein said that wormholes might connect parts of our own universe like an intergalactic expressway. However, there's no evidence that wormholes exist.

Albert Einstein (1879–1955)

Albert Einstein, one of the most famous scientists who ever lived, was such a brilliant, original thinker that his name has come to mean the same thing as "genius." His amazing theories of relativity gave people a completely new way to understand gravity, motion, and the way time and space are connected. Einstein's famous formula, $E=mc^2$, showed how energy could be changed into mass and vice versa. (The E means "energy," m means "mass," and c^2 is "the speed of light, squared.") Einstein's theories completely changed the way scientists think. In astronomy, they helped astronomers understand many cosmic mysteries, including the existence of black holes and the way gravity shapes the universe.

But Einstein's future didn't always look so bright. Born in Germany, young Albert didn't speak until he was three—he said he wanted to wait until he could speak in full sentences, but his parents thought that their child was backward. He dropped out of high school at the age of fifteen. Though he later earned his diploma and graduated from a university, he had a hard time finding a job. When he did finally find a position at a Swiss patent office, the absentminded scientist often dressed haphazardly, showing up to work in his green bedroom slippers and once wearing a piano runner as a scarf. Nevertheless, by the time of his death in 1955, Einstein had won the Nobel Prize in physics and was admired the world over.

Is there such a thing as extraterrestrial life?

Exobiologists, scientists who study the possibility of life on other planets, know that life could exist in places that are very different from Earth. The discovery of life-forms in unexpected places on Earth—in hot springs and pitch-black deep-sea vents—encourages us to think that creatures may thrive in places we once thought were hostile to life.

Extraterrestrial life is any form of life that might have begun beyond Earth's atmosphere. So far, scientists haven't met any extraterrestrials, or ETs—you'd have heard about it if they had! But we only began looking for life within our solar system about a hundred years ago and outside our solar system about forty years ago. Astronomers first discovered a planet orbiting a faraway star in 1992, and at least fifty more *extrasolar* (outside our Sun) planets have been detected since then. None of these planets is like ours, but with new planets being discovered every year, the possibility of life beyond Earth seems greater than ever.

But finding other planets doesn't necessarily mean we have intelligent galactic neighbors. First of all, a faraway planet must be able to support life. That life-form would have to evolve into *intelligent* life, and that intelligent life would have to build the technology to communicate across space. Phew! Life seems even more special than usual when you think of it in those terms!

We search for intelligent extraterrestrial life by:

a. sending a family picture into space

b. giving announcements over the Universal loudspeaker

c. searching the sky with enormous alien-detecting telescopes

d. listening to the most popular would-be alien radio stations

e. all of the above

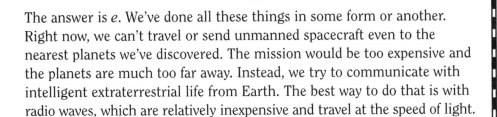

The answer is *e*. We've done all these things in some form or another. Right now, we can't travel or send unmanned spacecraft even to the nearest planets we've discovered. The mission would be too expensive and the planets are much too far away. Instead, we try to communicate with intelligent extraterrestrial life from Earth. The best way to do that is with radio waves, which are relatively inexpensive and travel at the speed of light.

Have we heard any alien rock bands?

Not yet, but we're trying. The Search for Extraterrestrial Intelligence, or SETI, began in 1960 when American astronomer Frank Drake used a radio telescope to listen for signals from two nearby, sunlike stars. Drake's receiver listened only on one radio frequency, but today organizations like the SETI Institute and the Planetary Society use more telescopes and search millions of radio frequencies. To detect an alien radio signal, we'll have to point a receiver in just the right direction and tune to just the right frequency—and there are billions of frequencies and billions of stars that might have planets around them.

In the meantime, we've sent our own message. In 1974, astronomers Carl Sagan and Frank Drake used the largest radio telescope in the world to broadcast a message about humans and Earth. The message was sent to a star cluster 24,000 light-years away, so we're not expecting a reply anytime soon.

We've been broadcasting unintentionally to the universe for nearly a hundred years. That's because all the radio broadcasts ever made have, in part, escaped into space. They are now traveling outward among the stars. But it's doubtful that aliens will ever hear your favorite song or radio commercial, because the signals would probably be too weak and confused to make sense if they reached anyone.

Have we sent any pictures or written messages into space?

Yes, we put messages on board the *Pioneer* and *Voyager* space probes that visited the outer planets in the 1970s and 1980s before sailing out of the solar system. Just in case they meet anyone, the probes have greeting plaques that illustrate a man and a woman and Earth's position in the solar system and among the stars. The greetings on *Voyager 1* and *2* also include a videodisk of sights and sounds of Earth. If the spacecraft ever encounter intelligent life, aliens could listen to Bach or jackhammers and look at pictures of human birth and Arizona's Monument Valley. *Voyager 1* has enough fuel to stay in touch with us until about 2020. By then, it'll be 14 billion miles (23 billion km) away.

COSMIC SUPERSTARS:

Carl Sagan (1934–1996)

Carl Sagan was an astronomer and biologist who was fascinated by the possibility of life in other parts of the universe. Much of Sagan's life was spent trying to make contact with extraterrestrials. He once said, "I would be very ashamed of my civilization if we did not try to find out if there is life in outer space." As one of the founders of the American space program, he helped send probes to Venus, Mars, Jupiter, Saturn, Uranus, and Neptune. It was Sagan's idea, along with that of Frank Drake, to attach "greetings" to the *Pioneer* and *Voyager* spacecraft. But perhaps most importantly, Sagan brought the wonders of science to the general public. His book *Cosmos* was the most popular science book ever.

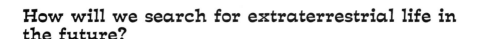

How will we search for extraterrestrial life in the future?

One way is with the Terrestrial Planet Finder (TPF), a special space observatory that the National Aeronautics and Space Administration (NASA) plans to launch in 2012. The TPF will look for planets orbiting nearby stars and study them for signs of life. Right now, planets orbiting other stars are hard to find because the bright glare from the star blocks them from our view. Usually astronomers find them because their gravity pulls on their parent star, making it wobble slightly. However, planets that are massive enough to do this and far enough away from their sun to be seen are not good candidates for life as we know it. The TPF will use many different kinds of telescopes at the same time to screen out the light produced by the stars, making smaller, more Earthlike planets visible.

CHAPTER 5

WILL HUMANS EVER LIVE ON OTHER WORLDS?

VOICES OF THE UNIVERSE

❝ I assume that life is capable of making itself at home in every corner of the universe, just as it has made itself at home in every corner of this planet. **❞**

—**Freeman Dyson**, British-American physicist

If stars and planets are so far away, how do we find out about them?

We have two ways of exploring space: by looking at it, and by visiting it. We can look at it with telescopes that detect the light, radio waves, X rays, and other radiation that come to us from space. We can visit it with spacecraft, both robotic and piloted. The last hundred years have seen huge progress in both these kinds of exploration.

Telescopes

With telescopes, is it "the bigger the better?"

It sure is. The bigger the telescope, the more light it captures and the farther and more you can see.

Some telescopes are built with lenses (these are *refracting telescopes*) and other are made with mirrors (*reflecting telescopes*). Reflecting telescopes can be made more powerful than refracting ones because a mirror can be supported from underneath, while a transparent glass lens must be supported from its edges—its thinnest and weakest part. But even mirrors can collapse under their own weight if they get too heavy. So some modern reflecting telescopes combine several smaller mirrors that act together as one.

George Ellery Hale (1868–1938)

American astronomer George Ellery Hale was determined to give the world bigger and better telescopes. He knew that the more powerful our telescopes were, the more we could learn about the universe. Hale spent forty years working to create a series of bigger and bigger telescopes, always demanding, "More light!" Little by little, he got it.

Hale's first project was raising the money to build a 40-inch refracting telescope, the world's largest, at Yerkes Observatory in Wisconsin. He then did the same thing for a 60-inch, and then a 100-inch, reflecting telescope at the observatory he co-founded at Mount Wilson, California. But Hale is best remembered for the 200-inch reflector that bears his name. The Hale Telescope, which began viewing the skies from California's Mount Palomar in 1948, was the world's largest reflector for 30 years.

What do you call an astronomer who's afraid of heights?

Unlucky! That's because the best observatories on Earth are built on top of mountains, where the air is usually clean and clear. The farther astronomers can get above factory smoke, car fumes, bright city lights, and even some of Earth's weather, the better. Even when the air is clean, Earth's windy atmosphere blurs the images we see of stars and planets. Astronomers want as little air between them and space as possible. In fact, some observatories are built on converted airplanes! Best of all are telescopes that can be sent into orbit around the Earth, where they are clear of our atmosphere altogether.

Why doesn't the Hubble Space Telescope fit the "bigger is better" rule?

The Hubble Space Telescope is the greatest telescope in the history of astronomy, yet it's not the biggest. That's because Hubble orbits Earth. In space, it can see farther and better than Earth-based scopes, even if they have larger mirrors. Since Hubble's launch in 1990, the telescope has revealed amazing things about outer space. It has even given us images of the distant reaches of the universe itself. Some of Hubble's observations include:

- pictures of the birth and death of stars

- evidence for supermassive black holes at the center of many galaxies

- images of the farthest galaxies we've ever seen

- the most detailed pictures of Pluto's moon, Charon

- dramatic scenes of the comet Shoemaker-Levy smashing into Jupiter in 1994

Why did the Hubble Space Telescope need surgery?

After Hubble was launched into space, scientists found that the telescope had a tiny—yet serious—flaw. The shape of the main mirror was off just a fraction of a hair's width, giving Hubble blurry vision. So astronauts flew into space in 1993 and pulled Hubble into the cargo bay of the space

shuttle. During thirty-five hours of careful space walks, they gave Hubble three new mirrors to act as a pair of "glasses." The astronauts' painstaking work paid off. Today Hubble's valuable pictures are crystal clear.

Will any telescope ever outdo Hubble?

If all goes as planned, when the Hubble Space Telescope retires in the first decade of this century, NASA will launch the Next Generation Space Telescope (NGST). Larger and more powerful than Hubble, the NGST promises to reveal parts of the universe even Hubble hasn't been able to see. Scientists hope to use the new telescope to observe the first stars and galaxies in the universe and learn how these bodies formed.

 ## Some telescopes resemble upside-down, opened-up umbrellas.

True. These are radio telescopes, or *radio dishes*. Radio telescopes use these huge dishes, instead of lenses, to collect radio waves. The dishes must be very large because radio waves are also very large. (The largest radio dish in the world, at the Arecibo Observatory in Puerto Rico, is bigger than three football fields.) Like the mirrors of reflecting telescopes, radio dishes can be combined to observe even larger portions of the sky.

Specialized telescopes that detect non-light types of radiation reveal all sorts of secrets about the universe. Some see X rays, while others detect gamma rays. Telescopes that see infrared light look through clouds of dust and gas in space to show us stars and galaxies that otherwise would have been hidden. Some reveal space objects, such as black holes and pulsars, that don't give off visible light. Each kind of telescope gives us a different view of the sky.

Many kinds of radiation cannot enter Earth's atmosphere. So most kinds of special telescopes must orbit outside our atmosphere the way the Hubble Space Telescope does.

Human Space Exploration

If you want to go to space, can you just fly an airplane higher and higher?

No. Airplanes aren't fast or powerful enough to escape Earth's atmosphere. To push hard enough to reach space, you need the power of a *rocket*. A rocket, in its simplest form, is a tube that holds fuel. When the fuel burns, gases shoot out the back of the tube, pushing the rocket forward. Rockets that propel spacecraft can push forward at more than 7 miles a second— that's more than 25,000 miles (40,000 km) per hour! At that rate, it takes only 8½ minutes to reach space.

 ## The rocket was invented more than 800 years ago.

True! (Though it wouldn't be used for spaceflight until much later.) Rockets were invented around the year 1150 by the Chinese, who had already invented gunpowder fireworks. These early rockets were handheld gunpowder arrows. They were used during celebrations and religious ceremonies and later during wars.

One story says that in the year 1500, Chinese scientist Wan Hu tied 47 rockets to his chair in hopes of creating a flying machine. (That was the end of test pilot Wan Hu.) Around the same time, in Italy, the famous artist and inventor Leonardo da Vinci (1452–1519) was also trying to build a flying machine. One of Leonardo's designs flapped its wings like a bird. Another looked like a helicopter with a huge propeller. Though Leonardo sketched and dreamed for twenty-five years, his wings never got off the ground.

It wasn't until about a hundred years ago that a Russian scholar named Konstantin Tsiolkovsky connected rockets to spaceflight. Tsiolkovsky worked out exactly what was needed to send a rocket to space, but he never built a rocket himself. That would be done by a scientist with a more hands-on approach, American Robert Goddard.

Robert Goddard (1882–1945)

Physicist Robert Goddard is known as the "father of American rocketry." As a child, Goddard was captivated by H. G. Wells's *War of the Worlds* (see page 48). He began designing rockets when he was still in school. When his idea of sending a rocket to the Moon was published in 1919, people mocked him by asking for rides there. The embarrassed scientist continued his work building rockets and experimenting with different fuels in private. Then in 1926, from his aunt's strawberry farm in Massachusetts, Goddard launched the first liquid-fueled rocket, a 10-foot-long device he called "Nell." It rose only 41 feet (12 m) in the air, about as high as the top of a two-story house, but it was the beginning of our journey to the Moon—and beyond.

Are space rockets powered by gunpowder?

No, and astronauts are probably glad about that. Modern rockets, like the ones used for the space shuttle, burn solid and liquid fuels during launch and only liquid fuel after launch. Solid fuel is easier to store, but liquid fuel can be turned on and off like a faucet.

The shuttle's solid fuel is a kind of aluminum that burns in a carefully controlled way. Its liquid fuel is liquid hydrogen, which combines with liquid oxygen. Sometimes the rocket launcher has several *stages*, or separate sections filled with fuel, one on top of the other. That way when one stage is used up, it can just fall away (usually into the ocean, where it is recovered), making the spacecraft lighter so it can travel faster.

All spacecraft are launched by a rocket. Once spacecraft and satellites are in orbit around Earth, the laws of nature keep them moving. When a spacecraft needs to change direction or return to Earth, it uses rockets called *thrusters*.

Does science fiction ever become science fact?

Some science fiction stories *have* actually predicted the future. The first ideas about space rocketry, for example, were inspired by the science-fiction tales of French author Jules Verne (1828–1905). In Verne's *From the Earth to the Moon* and *Around the Moon*, a three-man crew was launched into space with a cannon. Aside from the cannon, Verne described with amazing accuracy many aspects of spaceflight and travel—

more than 100 years before such a feat would become reality. Verne's stories inspired many people to study science, including Russian rocketry pioneer Konstantin Tsiolkovsky.

Was the Space Race an Olympic event?

No. *The Space Race* was an unofficial competition between the United States and the former Soviet Union (now Russia and some neighboring countries) to see which nation could be first to discover new things about space.

By the 1950s, rockets had become powerful enough to launch an object into orbit. The United States planned to be the first country to send an artificial satellite to space. (A *satellite* is anything that orbits Earth or another body in space; satellites can be natural, like a moon, or artificial, like the machines we use to send TV, radio, and telephone signals around the world.) But the Soviets surprised the Americans by launching their own satellite, *Sputnik 1*, in 1957. Tiny *Sputnik*, a radio-transmitting steel ball just 23 inches (58 cm) across, started the race for knowledge and power that brought us into the Space Age.

You use satellites every day.

If you listen to a weather forecast, talk on a cellular phone, or write to a faraway penpal using e-mail, the answer is *true*. Satellites today relay information from one part of Earth to another. Nearly all our long-distance radio, television, telephone, and Internet communications rely on satellites that orbit Earth. Satellites are also helpful in gathering information about our planet and atmosphere. From their viewpoint in space, satellites can create maps of Earth (including of the bottoms of the oceans!), rescue lost travelers by pinpointing any location on the globe, help us make weather forecasts, and can even let us spy on other countries. The Space Race wasn't just about being the first into space; it was also a way to discover how we could use space to improve our lives on Earth.

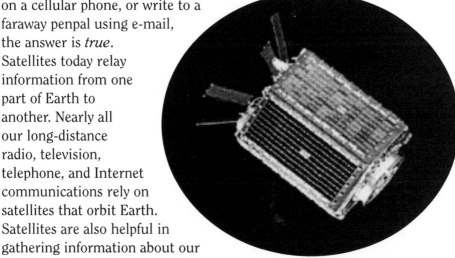

▲ This 705-pound U.S. Air Force/Phillips Laboratory satellite glides through space.

Who "won" the Space Race?

Nobody and everybody. Neither the United States nor the Soviet Union won the race because competition between them fizzled in the 1970s. Soon afterward, the two powers began to share projects and ideas. The things they learned about space and how to live there have helped everybody interested in space science.

But that doesn't mean that each nation didn't have times when it looked like it

Since *Sputnik 1*, more than 4,000 satellites have been launched into space. By 2001, about 1,300 of them had spent their fuel and fallen back toward Earth, burning up in our atmosphere. Of those that are left in space, only about 900 are still working.

was winning. The Soviets took the early lead, becoming the first to land a probe on the Moon, in 1959; to put a human in space, in 1961; and to send a person on a space walk outside a spacecraft, in 1965. The Americans finally got the upper hand when they landed the first person on the Moon, in 1969. Do you know that man's name? If not, turn to page 113.

Whose space is outer space?

▲ American and Soviet crewmen in front of a mockup of one of the spacecraft used in the Apollo Soyuz Test project. From left are astronauts Vance Brand and Thomas P. Stafford, cosmonauts Aleksey Leonov and Valeriy Kubasov, and astronaut Donald K. Slayton.

Everyone's. International law says that space and all the bodies in it are resources to be shared, used, and explored peacefully by everyone. The United States and the Soviet Union started the first cooperative space venture in 1975. These former rivals launched spacecraft that docked in space for two days. The astronauts shook hands on live TV and conducted experiments together.

Yuri Gagarin (1934–1968)

Yuri Gagarin was a Soviet Air Force pilot who had joined the cosmonaut (Soviet astronaut) training program. On his historic flight in 1961, the 27-year-old Gagarin orbited Earth once inside his spacecraft, *Vostok I*, and was home within 108 minutes.

Though it wasn't known at the time, the world later learned that there were problems on reentry and Gagarin survived only because he ejected himself and parachuted two miles into the ocean. Gagarin became a world hero. He traveled around the globe, was honored by the Soviet leader, Nikita Khrushchev, and given the title Hero of the Soviet Union. Gagarin died in 1968 when his jet crashed during a training flight for another space mission. His hometown, Klushino, was renamed Gagarin City.

VOICES OF THE UNIVERSE

" The stars appeared motionless, the Sun sewn on to black velvet. The only thing that moved was the Earth. **"**

—**Cosmonaut Alexei Leonov,** the first person to go on a space walk

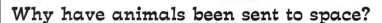

Why have animals been sent to space?

Not as pets (though they might go someday). Animals went to space before people did, serving as test pilots who made sure space and rocket travel would be safe for humans. In the 1950s, no one knew what would happen to living things in space. Scientists wanted as much information as possible before sending a human there. So "dognauts" and "chimpnauts" were recruited as the first true space pioneers.

The first animal in space was a Soviet dog named Laika, who traveled aboard *Sputnik II* in 1957. America's National Aeronautics and Space Administration, or NASA, put chimpanzees into orbit in 1959. One chimp, Ham, spent a year training for his flight! Today creatures from bees to bullfrogs to jellyfish to rats become space cadets so astronauts can study their behavior and the effects of weightlessness.

Did we send animals all the way to the Moon?

UNIVERSAL LANGUAGE

The word *astronaut* is Greek for "sailor of the stars."

No. We sent space probes, which could gather and send back the information we needed before we tried to land a human there. Between 1959 and 1969, dozens of Soviet and American spacecraft circled the Moon, took pictures of it, mapped its surface, and gathered rock and soil samples. Seven American *Surveyor* spacecraft also practiced landing on the Moon to make sure that a manned spacecraft wouldn't sink into its surface.

At the same time, both the United States and the Soviet Union were sending astronauts into orbit on longer and longer missions. They wanted to make sure astronauts could survive in space for the amount of time it would take to get to the Moon and back.

If all the animals stayed at home, how did an Eagle get to the Moon?

Eagle was the nickname for the lunar module of *Apollo 11*, the first spacecraft to land people on the Moon. History was made on July 20, 1969, when American astronauts Neil Armstrong and Edwin "Buzz" Aldrin detached *Eagle* from *Apollo 11*'s command module, *Columbia*, where a third astronaut, Michael Collins, remained. *Eagle* descended to the landing site and soon Armstrong and Aldrin became the first humans to set foot on another world. Many people have called the lunar landing the greatest scientific accomplishment of the modern world.

During their 21 hours and 36 minutes on the Moon, Armstrong and Aldrin put up an American flag and commemorative plaque, talked to then-President Richard Nixon via radio, took pictures, set up scientific experiments, and collected rock samples for scientists to study back on

Earth. When they were done, the top half of *Eagle* carried the moonwalkers back to their companion in *Columbia*. The lower part of *Eagle* was the launch platform and stayed on the Moon.

The flag that Armstrong and Aldrin put up on the Moon is fixed with a rod to look like it's waving in the breeze. But it isn't, because there's no air, and no wind, on the Moon!

COSMIC SUPERSTARS:

Neil Armstrong (1930–)

When Neil Armstrong was just two years old, his parents began taking him to the airport so he could watch airplanes take off and land. Neil started making model airplanes when he was about eight. He later used the money from his high school job to pay for his own flying lessons. Neil celebrated his sixteenth birthday by getting his pilot's license—even before he had a driver's license. The first person to set foot on the Moon is best remembered for his first words as he stepped from *Eagle*: "That's one small step for man, one giant leap for mankind."

What's it like to walk on the Moon?

Armstrong and Aldrin said it was easier than they expected. Walking on the Moon is more like bouncing on a trampoline than walking, since on the Moon you weigh only ⅙ of what you weigh on Earth. Once you get moving, it's hard to stop. You have to dig your heels into the dust and lean way back. You hope not to fall down when you do that, because even though you'd fall in slow motion and land softly in the gray moondust, getting up in that bulky space suit wouldn't be easy. Since the *Apollo* astronauts couldn't bend very well in their suits, they used special long-handled tongs to collect Moon rocks.

Astronauts' footprints will stay in the Moon's fine dust for millions of years, since the Moon has no wind or rain to erase them.

POP QUIZ: How many people have landed on the Moon?

- **a** 2
- **b** 12
- **c** 50
- **d** 300

The answer is *b*. Between 1969 and 1972, six *Apollo* missions landed twelve people (all American, all men) on the Moon. After the first landing, astronauts concentrated on doing scientific studies and exploring the Moon's different landscapes.

▲ Lunar module on the Moon's surface

On the last three *Apollo* missions, astronauts drove around in lunar rovers, or moon buggies. Though the rovers only had a top speed of 11 miles an hour (18 km per hour), they allowed the astronauts to cover more distance than they could on foot. The rover riders didn't travel any farther than 6 miles (10 km) from the landing site. If they had gone any farther and the rover had broken down, it would have been too far to walk back.

What planets have humans been to?

None, though there are plans to send astronauts to Mars. The best way for us to explore the planets and other distant, dangerous places right now is with space probes. Space probes are our robotic eyes and sensors. They take pictures, measure temperatures and wind speeds, and find out which chemicals surround them. Some space probes are designed to study space objects by flying around them, while others actually land on a planet's or moon's surface. Every probe is monitored

The lunar missions weren't *all* work and no play. Astronaut Alan Shepard, commander of the *Apollo 14* mission, celebrated his journey by hitting golf balls with a makeshift club. He said the balls flew "for miles and miles" in the low lunar gravity. Along with Shepard's two golf balls, lunar litter includes three Moon buggies, six American flags, six lunar landers, and one photo of an astronaut's family.

and controlled from Earth like a remote-controlled car. Space probes have visited the Sun, Moon, asteroids, comets, and every planet except Pluto. They have given us much of our information about the solar system.

 ## People live in space.

True. Astronauts live for months at a time aboard *space stations*, which are mini laboratories that orbit Earth. The first space station, the Soviet *Salyut*, was launched in 1971. Most space stations have been Russian, including *Mir*, which orbited Earth longer than any other space station. *Mir* hosted astronauts from many nations, including the United States, since it was launched in 1986. By the end of 2000, however, Russian officials were considering bringing the aging station down to Earth in a forced crash landing in the ocean.

What takes 16 countries, 45 space missions, and 850 hours of space walks?

▲ The International Space Station, as photographed by the Space Shuttle *Atlantis*

The construction of the International Space Station, which is going on above your head even as you read this. The United States and many other countries (Russia, Japan, Brazil, Canada, and eleven countries of the European Space Agency) are working together to build this permanent space station. It will take 45 separate space shuttle launches and at least 850 hours of space walks over five years. When the station is finished in 2004, it will be as big as fourteen tennis courts and will be the brightest object in the night sky after the Moon and Venus. Up to seven people will live on the Space Station at a time for a few months each. Crew members will research new high-tech products that could be made in weightlessness and used in medicine, computers, and as building materials.

Why do astronauts have to exercise on board space stations?

Space stations have taught us a lot about the effects of living in weightlessness for long periods of time. Since humans were meant to live in Earth's gravity, the zero gravity of space causes some dangerous problems. Without the pressure of gravity, astronauts' bones, hearts, and muscles become weaker because they don't have to work as hard to do their jobs. The astronauts also lose red blood cells, which deliver oxygen to the body. To make their hearts pump harder and keep their muscles and bones strong, astronauts must exercise every day.

Will humans ever live on other worlds?

Maybe; there might be a human settlement on Mars in this century. But even more likely in the near future is a research base on the Moon. People at a lunar base could study the Moon, or they could build a low-gravity launching pad for space probes or for training missions to Mars. Astronomers would also like to put telescopes on the far side of the Moon, where they'd have a fabulous view of the stars. Since the Moon has no atmosphere or city lights to get in the way, there's nothing to spoil the view.

A lunar base, which NASA has been planning to build since the 1960s, is becoming more of a reality all the time. There may be water ice at the Moon's poles, which would make Moon settlements much easier. The ice could be melted for drinking, washing, and growing plants. (It would be very costly to carry water from Earth.) American astronauts and Russian cosmonauts working together on *Mir* have managed to grow plants for food in zero gravity, which is important because space colonies would have to be able to feed and support themselves.

Some countries are also thinking of building hotels on the Moon and Mars. The hotels would be bases for space walks, sightseeing tours, and games and sports that can only be played in low gravity or weightlessness.

Do space shuttles explore other planets?

No. Though space shuttles can serve as short-term space laboratories, they're really built to do just what their name says—shuttle people and equipment back and forth to space. Space shuttles launch, retrieve, and repair satellites. They also carry crews and supplies to (and garbage from) *Mir* and the International Space Station.

The shuttles are different from most spacecraft because they're reusable.

Space shuttles sometimes recover broken satellites or other discarded items. Not only do we not want space to turn into a junkyard, but even the smallest pieces of space litter can be dangerous. For instance, a tiny piece of space junk—maybe no bigger than a paint chip—once damaged a space shuttle window. Many of the items floating in space will fall into Earth's atmosphere and burn up like meteors, but some are far enough away that they will stay in space for hundreds of years.

That saves a lot of money—imagine if you had to buy a new car every time you went on a family vacation! Engineers are now trying to design a reusable spaceplane that would take off and land on runways just like a regular plane, instead of taking off vertically like the space shuttle.

Why was the American space program put on hold in the 1980s?

Because of an awful disaster. The space shuttle *Challenger* had just taken off for its tenth flight in January 1986 when it exploded in the air and killed all seven people inside. Millions of people around the world were watching the liftoff because schoolteacher Christa McAuliffe was on board. McAuliffe, who'd been chosen to be the first teacher in space, was planning to broadcast lessons directly to schools from the shuttle's orbit around Earth.

The *Challenger* disaster led NASA to stop all space shuttle missions for nearly three years while they looked for the cause of the explosion and fixed the problem. They soon discovered that the shuttle had a faulty seal on one of the rocket boosters. Unfortunately, the teacher-in-space program was indefinitely put on hold. So were NASA's plans to send musicians, journalists, and artists to space.

Was *Challenger* the first tragic space mission?

No. Space travel is dangerous, and for all the successful space missions, there have been unsuccessful ones and many close calls. The first and worst disaster, a gigantic rocket explosion on a Soviet launchpad in 1960, killed 165 workers. The United States had a launchpad tragedy seven years later when a fire erupted during a launchpad test of *Apollo 1*. The three astronauts inside the spacecraft died because they could not get out.

The first death during an actual spaceflight happened when the parachute on a Soviet capsule became tangled on reentry, causing the capsule to crash and killing the cosmonaut inside. The only deaths in space to date have been three cosmonauts aboard the *Soyuz 11* space capsule, where a valve broke open and released the spacecraft's oxygen. All three suffocated before they could return to Earth.

What's It Like to Be an Astronaut?

What kind of suit takes 45 minutes to put on?

A space suit. That's because the suit is a complete life-support system that gives an astronaut everything he or she needs to survive in space.

Space is a dangerous place for unprotected humans. There s no air to breathe and no food or water. Temperatures range from superhigh (250 °F, or 122 °C) in sunlight, to superlow (-250 °F, or -157 °C) in shade. There's also harmful radiation in space and so little natural pressure that an unprotected human's blood would boil.

To overcome all these things, astronauts wear space suits for launch, work outside the space shuttle, and the return trip to Earth. Inside the shuttle, they wear casual clothes like those you wear on Earth.

 Astronauts grow taller in space.

True. Astronauts grow 1 to 2 inches (2.5 to 5 cm) in space because their spines stretch out in weightlessness. (Their suits are built with this in mind, to give them room to grow.) Unfortunately for astronauts who'd like to be taller, they return to their normal heights once they're back on Earth.

Spacewalking astronauts can snack from an energy bar and water bag velcroed inside their helmets— they just bend their heads downward and take a bite or a sip. But one thing they can't do very well is scratch an itch. Wearing a pressurized suit is kind of like wearing an inflated tire or a coat of armor!

How is life different on board the space shuttle?

When the shuttle is in orbit, astronauts float all around the inside. They can stand on walls and ceilings and do somersaults in the air. That takes some getting used to! Everything else that's not tied down floats around with them, too—including liquids. Astronauts sip liquids through straws so their drinks don't float away in bubbles.

Food isn't quite as much of a problem, as long as it's sticky enough to stay in its container. Astronauts eat pretty much the same food they do on Earth, but some of it is dried to keep it lightweight and fresh; they add water before mealtime. When they go to the bathroom, they have to strap themselves in and turn on a special vacuum on the toilet. And when it's time for bed, astronauts use sleeping bags attached to the shuttle walls so they won't float around while they sleep.

Do you have to go to outer space to feel weightless?

No. You might not know it, but you've probably felt tiny moments of weightlessness right here on Earth. Astronauts are weightless in space not because there's no gravity but because, without the ground to stand on, they're allowed to do what gravity wants them to—fall toward the center of Earth. However, the forward movement of their craft as it orbits keeps them from actually crashing to Earth.

Your feeling of weight—that pressure on your feet—is really just the ground getting in the way of your fall. If you've ever ridden over a bump in the car, or on a rollercoaster that goes upside down, you've momentarily taken the ground away. When you feel your stomach fall a tiny bit later than the rest of your body, you're feeling weightless just like astronauts do!

How do astronauts prepare for weightlessness?

▲ Astronaut Mary Ellen Weber prepares for weightlessness in space.

They fly on a special jet they've named the "Vomit Comet." The jet, which has had all the seats taken out, flies down in an arc until just before it hits the ground. This lets the astronauts float in air for a short time. Before the jet reaches the ground, it zooms right back up, pinning the astronauts to the floor until the pilot repeats the trick—about 40 times before landing. You can see where the plane got its name!

Why are all the switches in the space shuttle cockpit so big?

Even though there are more than 1,000 switches, controls, and computer displays that have to fit into the shuttle cockpit, the switches must allow for astronauts wearing space suits and bulky gloves. If the buttons were a normal size, moving the switches would be like trying to work a TV remote control while wearing ski gloves.

Who flies the space shuttle into orbit?

Nobody—the shuttle flies itself. Putting a shuttle into orbit requires following such a precise path that a computer autopilot steers the shuttle out of Earth's atmosphere. Though the astronauts can take over at any time, they would only do so in an emergency. For landing, the shuttle commander takes over from the autopilot with five or six minutes to go and lands the shuttle on the runway.

What sound does a space shuttle make in orbit?

No sound at all. That's because space is absolutely silent. Since there's no air in space, there's no way for sound to travel. Astronauts who are spacewalking outside the shuttle have to use radios inside their helmets to talk to one another, even when they're standing only inches apart.

Can astronauts call home when they're in space?

Astronauts on missions of ten days or more get one private 15-minute phone call with their families. The calls are made via two-way radio. The space shuttle can also receive faxes and e-mail, but only from Mission Control. Soon you'll probably be able to e-mail astronauts in orbit. Maybe one day, it'll be you getting the e-mail on your way to the space station, Mars—or beyond.

Milestones in the Universe

B.C.

4241 The Egyptian calendar, the first known to be based on 365 days, is created.

c. 3000 The Babylonians predict eclipses.

2296 Chinese observers make the earliest known recorded comet sighting.

c. 1900–1600 Stonehenge is built in Britain, probably as a huge calculator to chart the movements of the Sun, Moon, and planets.

c. 1750 Babylonians put together star catalogs and planetary records.

c. 1600 Astrologers in Mesopotamia identify the constellations of the zodiac.

585 Thales of Miletus, in what is now Turkey, accurately predicts a solar eclipse. Because the eclipse is taken as a bad sign, a nearby war is called off.

352 Chinese observers report a supernova, the earliest recorded sighting.

c. 350 Aristotle, the great Greek philosopher, states that Earth is the center of the universe.

c. 300 Chinese astronomers compile star maps that will be used for the next several hundred years.

c. 270 Aristarchus challenges Aristotle's teachings by saying the Sun is the center of the solar system.

c. 240 Eratosthenes, a Greek scholar, calculates the distance around the world at the equator, coming remarkably close to the present accepted value of 24,901 miles.

46 On the advice of Greek astronomer Sosigenes, Julius Caesar introduces a calendar of 365 days and a leap year every four years in Rome. This is now known as the Julian calendar.

A.D.

c. 140 Greek astronomer Ptolemy writes a collection of books, later called *Almagest*, which becomes the basis of astronomy for nearly 1,500 years.

832 "House of Wisdom" is founded in Baghdad. One of the many centers of learning that appeared in the Islamic empire, the center has an observatory and is the site where many Greek texts are translated into Arabic.

1066 A large comet is sighted during William the Conqueror's invasion of England. Today the comet is known as Halley's Comet.

1543 Nicolaus Copernicus's *De revolutionibus orbium coelestium* (*On the Revolutions of the Heavenly Spheres*) is published just before his death. The work proposes that the Sun is the center of the planets' orbits.

1584 Giordano Bruno's *Cena de la Ceneri* (*The Dinner of Ashes*) defends the Copernican view of the universe. For this, Bruno is burned at the stake by the Catholic Church in 1600.

1602 Tycho Brahe's *Introduction to the New Astronomy* is published after his death, containing the positions for 1,000 stars.

1603 German astronomer Johann Bayer introduces the method of naming stars within each constellation by Greek letters.

1608 Dutch eyeglass maker Hans Lippershey invents the telescope.

1609 Galileo Galilei begins building and refining telescopes.

Johannes Kepler's *New Astronomy* says that the planets revolve around the Sun in elliptical, not circular, orbits.

1610 Galileo points his telescope at the sky, changing our view of the universe forever. He reports his findings of Jupiter's moons, Saturn's rings, and the phases of Venus in *Siderius Nuncius* (*Starry Messenger*).

1616 Galileo receives warning from the Catholic Church not to defend Copernican theory; Copernicus's *De revolutionibus* is placed on the *Index* (list of banned books) of the church, from which it is not removed until 1835.

1619 Kepler's *Epitome of Copernican Astronomy* defends Copernican theory and is immediately placed on the *Index*.

Kepler explains that comets' tails always point away from the Sun because of the solar wind.

1632 Galileo's *Dialogo sopra i due massimi sistemi del mondo* (*Dialogue Concerning the Two Chief World Systems*) represents his pro-Copernican view and angers the church; the book is placed on the *Index*.

1633 The Catholic Inquisition forces Galileo to take back his view that Earth moves around the Sun.

1642 Galileo dies in Italy; Isaac Newton is born in England.

1656 Dutch mathematician and astronomer Christian Huygens discovers that the "ears" Galileo saw on Saturn are really rings. He also discovers Saturn's biggest moon, Titan.

1682 Edmond Halley observes the comet that will later be named after him.

1687 Isaac Newton produces his most famous work, the *Principia*, which describes his three laws of motion and the law of universal gravitation.

1781 William Herschel discovers the planet Uranus, which he at first believes to be a comet.

1801 Giuseppe Piazzi discovers the first asteroid, Ceres.

1839 Harvard College Observatory, the first official observatory in the United States, is founded.

1849   Hippolyte Fizeau measures the speed of light to within 5 percent of today's accepted value of 186,000 miles per second.

1865   Jules Verne's novel *From the Earth to the Moon* features men being sent to the Moon by cannon.

1877   Giovanni Schiaparelli discovers "channels" on Mars.

1887   The world's first mountaintop telescope is installed on Mt. Hamilton near San Francisco, CA.

1903   Russian rocketry pioneer Konstantin Tsiolkovsky proposes that liquid fuel can be used for space travel.

1905   Albert Einstein submits his first paper on the special theory of relativity.

1908   A mysterious explosion in the Tunguska region of Siberia, Russia, flattens millions of trees and sends shock waves around the world. Possible causes include an asteroid hitting Earth.

1911   A basketball-sized meteorite kills a dog in Egypt, the only recorded case of a meteorite killing an animal.

1914   American Robert Goddard begins to develop experimental rockets.

1915   Albert Einstein completes his general theory of relativity, containing the idea that space and time cannot be separated.

1916   Astronomer Karl Schwarzschild uses Einstein's theories to describe a theoretical black hole.

1922   Russian Alexander Friedman predicts that the universe is expanding.

1926   Robert Goddard launches the first liquid-fuel rocket.

1927   In the first version of the Big Bang theory, Belgian priest Georges Lemaître proposes that the universe was created in an explosion of matter and energy.

1929 Edwin Hubble determines that the farther away a galaxy is, the faster it is moving away from us, confirming that the universe is expanding.

1930 Clyde Tombaugh discovers the planet Pluto.

1934 German engineer Wernher von Braun develops a liquid-fuel rocket that flies 1.5 miles (2.4 km) into the air.

1949 The first rocket with more than one stage reaches a height of 240 miles (386 km).

1957 The Soviet Union launches the first artificial satellite, *Sputnik*, into space.

The Soviet Union launches *Sputnik 2*, which carries the first Earthling, a dog named Laika, into space.

1958 The U.S. launches its first successful satellite, *Explorer I*.

1959 The first of twenty-four Soviet *Luna* probes begins exploring the Moon.

1961 Soviet cosmonaut Yuri Gagarin becomes the first person in space when he orbits Earth aboard *Vostok I*. United States President John F. Kennedy vows that America will land a human on the Moon by the end of the decade.

Astronaut Alan B. Shepard Jr. becomes the first American in space when his *Mercury 3* capsule *Freedom 7* completes a 15-minute suborbital flight.

1962 The U.S. space probe *Mariner 2* reaches Venus, becoming the first machine from Earth to travel to another planet.

John Glenn Jr. is the first American to orbit Earth in his capsule *Friendship 7*.

Telstar, the first active communications satellite, is launched. It relays the first transatlantic television pictures.

1963 Soviet cosmonaut Valentina Tereshkova becomes the first woman in space.

1965   Soviet cosmonaut Alexei Leonov takes the first "space walk" outside his spacecraft.

1966   The Soviet space probe *Luna 9* makes the first soft (not crash) landing on the Moon.

1967   American astronauts Virgil "Gus" Grissom, Edward White, and Roger Chaffee die in a fire during a ground test of *Apollo 1*.

   Soviet cosmonaut Vladimir Komarov dies when his spacecraft's parachute gets tangled on reentry and the craft crashes.

1968   America's *Surveyor VII* becomes the first space vehicle to land undamaged on the Moon.

   The three-man crew of America's *Apollo 8* spacecraft becomes the first to escape Earth's gravitational field and orbit the Moon.

1969   *Apollo 11* lands on the Moon; American astronaut Neil Armstrong becomes the first person to walk on the Moon, with crewmember Edwin "Buzz" Aldrin right behind him. Michael Collins orbits above.

1971   The Soviets launch *Salyut 1*, the world's first space station.

1972   American space probe *Pioneer 10* is launched; in 1983 it becomes the first probe to leave the solar system.

1973   The first American space station, *Skylab*, goes into orbit.

1975   In the first cooperative space venture between the United States and the Soviet Union, a three-man American crew docks with a two-man Soviet crew in space.

1976   The U.S. *Viking* space probes land on Mars and begin sending pictures back to Earth.

   U.S. space probes *Voyager 1* and *Voyager 2* are launched to Jupiter and the other gas giants.

1980 The Very Large Array (VLA) radio telescope, a group of twenty-seven radio dishes that span more than 11 miles (17 km) on Earth, begins operation in Socorro, New Mexico.

Voyager 1 and *Voyager 2* fly past Saturn, gathering information about the planet, its moons, and its rings.

1981 The U.S. spacecraft *Columbia* is the first to be reused and sent on a second mission.

1983 Sally Ride becomes the first female American astronaut in space, flying aboard the space shuttle *Challenger*.

1985 Construction of the Keck telescope, the world's largest, begins on Maui, Hawaii.

1986 The space shuttle *Challenger* explodes 73 seconds after takeoff, killing the six astronauts and teacher Christa McAuliffe on board.

The Soviet *Mir*, the first permanently manned space station, is launched.

Voyager 2 is the first spacecraft to fly by Uranus.

Space probe *Giotto* takes close-up photographs of the head of Halley's Comet.

1989 *Voyager 2* is the first spacecraft to fly by Neptune.

1990 The Hubble Space Telescope becomes the first telescope to orbit at the edge of Earth's atmosphere.

1992 *Galileo* is the first spacecraft to visit the asteroid belt.

1997 Space probe *Pathfinder* lands on Mars and releases the remote-controlled buggy *Sojourner* to test for signs of life on the planet.

1998 Construction of the International Space Station begins.

Space probe *Prospector* confirms possible presence of water ice at the Moon's north and south poles.

GLOSSARY

absolute magnitude: the true brightness of a star as compared to other stars; calculated as if all stars were seen from a distance of 32.6 light-years from Earth.

apparent magnitude: the apparent brightness of a star as compared to other stars when seen from Earth.

asteroid: a small rocky body orbiting the Sun; sometimes called a "minor planet."

astrology: the belief that people's lives are affected by the movement of the stars and heavens.

astronomy: the scientific study of everything in the universe beyond Earth's atmosphere.

atmosphere: the outer layer of gases that surrounds a planet, moon, or star.

atom: the basic building block of the elements that make up all matter in the universe.

auroras: bright, often colored, displays of light in the sky caused by the solar wind interacting with Earth's electromagnetic fields.

axis: an imaginary line through the poles of a celestial body, around which the body rotates.

Big Bang: the moment 13 to 15 billion years ago when most scientists agree the universe began expanding from an incredibly dense speck.

black hole: a dead star whose gravity is so strong that nothing can escape it, not even light.

celestial: having to do with the sky.

Cepheid variables: stars that grow brighter and dimmer at very regular intervals, allowing astronomers to measure the stars' distance from Earth.

comet: a small body of ice and dust that orbits the Sun; when it travels close enough to the Sun to be warmed by the Sun's heat, it forms a tail of dust and gas that streams out into space.

constellation: one of eighty-eight recognized groups of stars that form a picture in the sky.

corona: the outer layer of the Sun's atmosphere.

cosmology: the study of the origins and structure of the universe.

crater: a round, shallow hole in the surface of a celestial body, made by the impact of incoming asteroids and meteoroids.

electromagnetic spectrum: the range of electromagnetic radiation separated by wavelength into gamma rays, X rays, ultraviolet (UV) rays, visible light rays, infrared waves, and radio waves.

event horizon: the outer edge of a black hole that is the last place light, gas, and matter can be detected.

extraterrestrial: anything that originates beyond Earth's atmosphere.

galaxy: a collection of millions to trillions of stars held together by their own gravitational attraction.

geocentric model: the theory that places Earth at the center of our solar system.

gravity: a force that pulls all objects toward each other; the greater an object's mass, the greater its force of gravity.

greenhouse effect: the effect created in a planet's atmosphere by gases that trap the Sun's heat and warm the planet.

heavens: what the ancients called the part of the universe we can see from Earth.

heliocentric model: the theory that places the Sun at the center of our solar system.

hemisphere: half of a planet or other spherical celestial body.

light-year: the distance light travels in a year, or almost 6 trillion miles (9.5 trillion km).

luminosity: the measure of a star's energy output.

lunar eclipse: an event that occurs when Earth passes between the Moon and the Sun, darkening the Moon.

magnetic field: the natural magnetic force of a planet or other object.

mass: the amount of matter in an object.

matter: the material an object is made of.

meteor: a meteoroid that enters Earth's atmosphere and burns up in a streak of light.

meteorite: a meteoroid that survives the passage through Earth's atmosphere and lands on Earth's surface.

meteoroid: a piece of rock or dust in space.

moon: a body that travels around a planet.

nebula: a cloud of gas and dust found in space between stars; often the birthplace of new stars.

neutron star: a small, hot, spinning star that is the remains of a supernova.

nuclear fusion: the process of two atoms joining together under enormous pressure, resulting in a large release of energy; the source of power for the Sun and other stars.

orbit: the path of an object that revolves around another object.

planet: a large, round heavenly body that travels around a star.

pulsar: a very dense celestial body, probably a neutron star, that pulses with regular bursts of energy.

quasar: the extremely bright center of a very distant galaxy.

radiation: energy that travels through space as waves.

redshift: the increase in wavelength of radiation that happens when an object in space is moving away from the observer.

rocket: a machine that provides the power for spacecraft to escape Earth's atmosphere.

satellite: a natural or artificial object in orbit around another object.

scientific method: making a guess about something and experimenting to see if you're right.

solar eclipse: an event that occurs when the Moon passes between Earth and the Sun, blocking the Sun's light.

solar flare: an eruption on the Sun's surface caused by holes in the Sun's magnetic field.

solar system: a star and all the planets, moons, and other bodies that revolve around it.

solar wind: a steady stream of charged particles that flows out from the Sun's surface.

space probe: a spacecraft that is programmed to do experiments but doesn't carry people.

space shuttle: a reusable spacecraft that carries crews and equipment to space and back.

space station: an orbiting satellite in which crews live for extended periods of time to conduct research in space.

star: a large ball of hot gas that gives off light and heat because it generates nuclear energy deep within its core; the Sun is a star.

sunspot: a dark patch on the Sun's surface that is cooler than the rest of the Sun.

supernova: the superbright explosion of an old, very massive star.

universe: all of space and everything in it.

zodiac: an imaginary belt along the path of the Sun in the sky; the zodiac is divided into twelve parts, each of which is named after a different constellation.

SELECTED BIBLIOGRAPHY

Asimov, Isaac. *Isaac Asimov's Guide to Earth and Space*. New York: Ballantine Books, 1993.

———. *What Makes the Sun Shine?* Boston: Little, Brown, 1971.

———. *The Sun and Its Secrets*. Milwaukee: Gareth Stevens Publishing, 1994.

Beasant, Pam. *1000 Facts About Space*. New York: Larousse Kingfisher Chambers, 1992.

Becklake, Sue. *All About Space*. New York: Scholastic Reference, 1998.

Bond, Peter. *DK Guide to Space: A Photographic Journey Through the Universe*. New York: DK Publishing, 1999.

Branley, Franklyn. *Comets*. New York: Thomas Y. Crowell, 1984.

———. *Eclipse*. New York: Thomas Y. Crowell, 1988.

———. *Floating in Space*. New York: HarperCollins, 1998.

———. *Gravity Is a Mystery*. New York: HarperCollins, 1986.

———. *Shooting Stars*. New York: HarperCollins, 1983.

———. *What the Moon Is Like*. New York: HarperCollins, 1986.

Campbell, Ann-Jeanette. *Amazing Space*. New York: John Wiley & Sons, 1997.

Englebert, Phillis, and Diane Dupuis. *The Handy Space Answer Book*. Detroit: Visible Ink Press, 1998.

Fardon, John. *Dictionary of the Earth*. New York: Dorling Kindersley, 1994.

Gusch, William A. Jr. *1001 Things Everyone Should Know About the Universe*. New York: Doubleday, 1998.

Mitton, Jacqueline, and Simon Mitton. *Scholastic Encyclopedia of Space*. New York: Scholastic Reference, 1999.

Muirden, James. *Stars and Planets*. New York: Kingfisher Books, 1993.

Mullane, R. Mike. *Do Your Ears Pop in Space?* New York: John Wiley & Sons, 1997.

Oxford Dictionary of Scientists. New York: Oxford University Press, 1999.

Parker, Steve. *What If . . . Space*. Brookfield, Conn.: Copper Beech Books, 1995.

Petty, Kate. *I Didn't Know That the Sun Is a Star*. Brookfield, Conn.: Copper Beech Books, 1997.

———. *I Didn't Know That You Can Jump Higher on the Moon*. Brookfield, Conn.: Copper Beech Books, 1997.

Random House Webster's Dictionary of Scientists. New York: Random House, 1997.

Redfern, Martin. *The Kingfisher Young People's Book of Space*. New York: Kingfisher Publications, 1998.

Ronan, Colin A. *The Universe Explained*. New York: Henry Holt, 1994.

Sagan, Carl. *Cosmos*. New York: Ballantine Books, 1980.

Segal, Justin. *The Amazing Space Almanac*. Los Angeles: Lowell House Juvenile, 1998.

Severance, John B. *Einstein: Visionary Scientist*. New York: Clarion Books, 1999.

Simon, Seymour. *Destination: Jupiter*. New York: Morrow Junior Books, 1998.

———. *Galaxies*. New York: Morrow Junior Books, 1988.

———. *Mars*. New York: Morrow Junior Books, 1987.

———. *Mercury*. New York: Morrow Junior Books, 1992.

———. *Our Solar System*. New York: Morrow Junior Books, 1992.

———. *Stars*. New York: Morrow Junior Books, 1986.

———. *The Sun*. New York: Morrow Junior Books, 1986.

———. *The Universe*. New York: Morrow Junior Books, 1998.

Stott, Carole. *I Wonder Why Stars Twinkle and Other Questions About Space*. New York: Kingfisher Books, 1993.

———. *Moon Landing: The Race for the Moon*. New York: Dorling Kindersley, 1999.

———. *Space Exploration*. New York: Alfred A. Knopf, 1997.

Trotman, Felicity. *Exploration of Space*. New York: Barron's Educational Series, 1998.

The Universe. Alexandria, Va.: Time-Life Books, 1998.

The Usborne First Guide to the Universe. London: Usborne Publishing, 1993.

INDEX

Native American names for, 44
possible hotels on, 118
possible research base on, 117–18
space probes of, 112, 128–30
tides and, 43
waning and waxing of, 43
moons
of asteroids, 65
of Jupiter, 52
of Neptune, 60
of Pluto, 63, 64, 104
of Saturn, 54, 55
in solar system, number of, 28
of Uranus, 58

−N−

NASA (National Aeronautics and
Space Administration), 101, 105,
112, 118
Native Americans, 44, 78
Neptune, 26, 62, 130
description of, 58–60
rings of, 54, 60
neutrinos, 96
neutron stars, 83–86
Newton, Sir Isaac, 24, 26, 88, 126
Next Generation Space Telescope
(NGST), 105
Nixon, Richard, 113
North Star (Polaris), 81
novas, 84–85. *See also* supernovas
nuclear fusion, 27, 96

−O−

omega amount of matter, 95
Oort Cloud, 66
open universe model, 95
optical doubles, 79

−P−

Pandora, 54
Pathfinder spacecraft, 50, 130
penumbra, 45
period, definition of, 66
Phoebe, 55
photosphere, 30

Pioneer space probes, 100, 129
Planetary Society, 99
planets
discovered by mathematics, 59, 62
extrasolar, 98–99, 101
gas giants, 27
gravity of, 25–26
number of, 28
orbits of, 23, 26, 125
origin of name of, 15
rings of, 54, 57, 60
stars compared to, 72–73
plants, growing of, in space, 118
Plato, 12
Pluto, 23, 25–27, 52, 128
description of, 61–64
Pluto-Kuiper Express space probe, 63
Polaris (North Star), 81
prime mover (God), 15, 16
Prometheus, 54
protostars, 72
Proxima Centauri, 74
Ptolemy (Claudius Ptolemaeus),
16–17, 21, 80, 125
pulsars, 85, 105

−Q−

quasars, 93

−R−

radiation, 77
from neutron stars, 85
redshift in wavelength of, 91
telescopes and detection of, 105
radiative zone (of Sun), 30
radio dishes (radio telescopes), 99,
105, 130
radios in space, 123
radio waves, 77, 85, 93
in search for extraterrestrial
intelligence, 99
red giants, 83
redshift, 91
relativity, theories of, 97, 127
Ride, Sally, 130
Rimbaud, Arthur, 27

Kenneth C. Davis is the *New York Times* best-selling author of DON'T KNOW MUCH ABOUT® HISTORY, DON'T KNOW MUCH ABOUT® GEOGRAPHY, DON'T KNOW MUCH ABOUT® THE CIVIL WAR, AND DON'T KNOW MUCH ABOUT® THE BIBLE.

People magazine has said that "Reading [Davis] is like returning to the classroom of the best teacher you ever had."

A frequent visitor to classrooms and teacher groups, Davis has appeared often on *The Today Show*, *Good Morning America*, CNN, National Public Radio, and many other television and radio shows. He is a contributing editor to *USA Weekend*, which features his Don't Know Much About® quizzes on a variety of subjects. Born and educated in Mt. Vernon, New York, he now lives in New York City and Vermont with his wife, Joann, and their two children, Jenny and Colin.